Enhancing the Role of Government in the Pacific Island Economies

The World Bank
Washington, D.C.

World Bank Country Studies are among the many reports originally prepared for internal use as part of the continuing analysis by the Bank of the economic and related conditions of its developing member countries and of its dialogues with the governments. Some of the reports are published in this series with the least possible delay for the use of governments and the academic, business and financial, and development communities. The typescript of this paper therefore has not been prepared in accordance with the procedures appropriate to formal printed texts, and the World Bank accepts no responsibility for errors. Some sources cited in this paper may be informal documents that are not readily available.

The findings, interpretations, and conclusions expressed in this paper are entirely those of the author(s) and should not be attributed in any manner to the World Bank, to its affiliated organizations, or to members of its Board of Executive Directors or the countries they represent. The World Bank does not guarantee the accuracy of the data included in this publication and accepts no responsibility for any consequence of their use. The boundaries, colors, denominations, and other information shown on any map in this volume do not imply on the part of the World Bank Group any judgment on the legal status of any territory or the endorsement or acceptance of such boundaries.

Map illustration by Karen Siatras, Meadows Design Office Inc., Washington, D.C. (www.mdomedia.com).

ISSN: 0253-2123

Library of Congress Cataloging-in-Publication Data

Enhancing the role of government in the Pacific Island economies.
       p.   cm. — (A World Bank country study)
    Includes bibliographical references.
    ISBN 0-8213-4351-3
    1. Islands of the Pacific—Economic policy.   2. Islands of the
Pacific—Social policy.   3. Government spending policy—Islands of
the Pacific.   4. Finance, Public—Islands of the Pacific—
Accounting.   5. Total quality management in government—Islands of
the Pacific.   I. World Bank.   II. Series.
HC681.E545   1998
338.99—dc21
                                                            98-45139
                                                              CIP

CONTENTS

Map: IBRD 29631

List of Tables

List of Figures

List of Boxes

List of Charts

ABSTRACT

This report discusses how the Pacific Islands development agenda could be put into practice by improving the effectiveness of government activities in nine Pacific Island countries that are members of the World Bank (PMCs)—Fiji, Kiribati, Federated States of Micronesia, Marshall Islands, Republic of Palau, Samoa, Solomon Islands, Tonga and Vanuatu.

The report analyzes the scope of government in the PMCs, their spending patterns and priorities, and the budgetary processes that give rise to spending choices. It is structured along three interlinking themes about enhancing the role of government: (i) to focus on core functions, match government tasks to its capacity, and to improve public sector accountability; (ii) to raise the efficiency of public sector spending through policies designed to quicken the pace of economic growth and reduce poverty; and (iii) to implement planning and budgetary procedures within the framework of a medium-term development horizon and to improve processes of public spending, including those programs financed through external aid. The report also includes nine country profiles.

ACKNOWLEDGMENTS

The World Bank wishes to express its appreciation to all member Governments, bilateral donor agencies, the Asian Development Bank, the Forum Secretariat, the International Monetary Fund, the United Nations Development Programme, the East-West Center, University of Hawaii, the Bank of Hawaii, and several research organizations, non-governmental organizations and individuals for their cooperation in preparing this report. The World Bank acknowledges, in particular, the valuable support for the study provided by the Australian Agency for International Development (AusAID).

This report was prepared by a team led by Hilarian Codippily, based on the field work carried out in late 1997. The core team included John Fallon (role of government), Hjordis Bierman (public finance), Geoffrey Dixon (planning and budgeting), Craig Sugden (structure and size of government), Lawrence Salmen and Caroline Robb (participatory development), and Peter Osei (country profiles). Navitalai Naisoro, Kolone Vaai, assisted by Maiava Peteru, and Joshua Levene were responsible for the participatory assessment surveys conducted in Fiji, Samoa and Tonga.

This report has benefited from major contributions by Richard Newfarmer and Michael Stevens, who was also a Peer Reviewer. Other Peer Reviewers were Vinay Swaroop, Hansjorg Elshorst, and Aubrey Williams. The report also benefited from the comments of Elizabeth Brouwer, Sofia Bettencourt, Stuart Whitehead, Wei Ding, Roland Kyle Peters, Sylvia Ting, and research assistance from Vargha Azad. The report was prepared with guidance from Klaus Rohland. Bonita Brindley provided editorial advice and Ana Rivas and Andrea Doering assisted in the final stages of document processing. Lily Tsang provided administrative support and coordinated the processing of the report.

ACRONYMS AND ABBREVIATIONS

ADB	=	Asian Development Bank
A$	=	Australian Dollar
ALTA	=	Agricultural Landlords and Tenants Act
AusAID	=	Australian Agency for International Development
CDF	=	Commodity Development Framework
CEM	=	Country Economic Memorandum
CRP	=	Comprehensive Reform Programs
DB	=	Development Budget
EDI	=	Economic Development Institute
EEZ	=	Exclusive Economic Zone
FEA	=	Fiji Electricity Authority
FSM	=	Federated States of Micronesia
GDI	=	Gross Domestic Investment
GDP	=	Gross Domestic Product
IMF	=	International Monetary Fund
ICOR	=	Incremental Capital-Output Ratio
NBF	=	National Bank of Fiji
NGO	=	Non-Government Organization
NLTB	=	Native Land Trust Board
PMC	=	Pacific Island Member Country
PNG	=	Papua New Guinea
PSIP	=	Public Sector Investment Program
PUB	=	Public Utility Board
RER	=	Regional Economic Report
RERF	=	Revenue Equalization Reserve Fund
RMI	=	Republic of Marshall Islands
SI$	=	Solomon Islands Dollar
SPREP	=	South Pacific Regional Environment Programme
UNDP	=	United Nations Development Programme
US	=	United States
US$	=	United States Dollar
VAT	=	Valued Added Tax

Vice President:	Jean-Michel Severino
Director:	Klaus Rohland, EACNI
Sector Manager:	Masahiro Kawai, EASPR
Task Manager:	Hilarian Codippily, EASPR

CURRENCY EQUIVALENTS

FEDERATED STATES OF MICRONESIA (FSM)

(The U.S. Dollar is the official currency of exchange)

FISCAL YEAR

October 1 - September 30

FIJI

Annual Averages

1994   F$1.00 = US$0.68

1995   F$1.00 = US$0.71

1996   F$1.00 = US$0.71

1997   F$1.00 = US$0.69

FISCAL YEAR

January 1 - December 31

KIRIBATI

Annual Averages

(The Australian Dollar is the official currency and main medium of exchange)

1994   A$1.00 = US$0.73

1995   A$1.00 = US$0.74

1996   A$1.00 = US$0.78

1997   A$1.00 = US$0.74

FISCAL YEAR

January 1 - December 31

MARSHALL ISLANDS

(The U.S. Dollar is the official currency of exchange)

FISCAL YEAR

October 1 - September 30

SAMOA
Annual Averages
1994   Tala 1.00 = US$0.39

1995   Tala 1.00 = US$0.40

1996   Tala 1.00 = US$0.41

1997   Tala 1.00 = US$0.39

FISCAL YEAR
July 1 - June 30

SOLOMON ISLANDS
Annual Averages
1994   SI$1.00 = US$0.30

1995   SI$1.00 = US$0.29

1996   SI$1.00 = US$0.28

1997 SI$1.00 = US$0.27

FISCAL YEAR
January 1 to December 31

TONGA
Annual Averages
1994   T$1.00 = US$0.76

1995   T$1.00 = US$0.79

1996   T$1.00 = US$0.81

1997   T$1.00 = US$0.79

FISCAL YEAR
July 1 - June 30

VANUATU
Annual Averages
1994   Vt100 = US$0.86

1995   Vt100 = US$0.89

1996   Vt100 = US$0.90

1997   Vt100 = US$0.90

FISCAL YEAR
January 1 - December 31

EXECUTIVE SUMMARY

Pacific Island governments are increasingly aware that state-led growth, based upon high levels of public investment and financed with aid flows, has not substantially increased per capita incomes, or quality of life. The East Asian financial crisis has added to the sense of *malaise* in the Pacific. Although the full impact of the East Asian financial crisis on the Pacific Island Member Countries (PMCs) is not yet known, it appears to be pushing them into recession. Building a more resilient economic base has become a matter of political urgency.

Economic Performance. In the PMCs, per capita real GDP growth has been much lower than in other island economies in the Caribbean, African, or Indian Oceans. Although the PMCs had invested about 29 percent of GDP in their economies during the 1980s, economic growth clung persistently to around 2 percent per year. GDP growth improved slightly to 3.1 percent per year in 1992-96, but the overall returns to investment remains low. Average economic growth rates appear to have turned sharply negative since the onset of the East Asian financial crisis. The Pacific Islands need to diversify their production bases and export markets as well as exercise greater prudential supervision over their respective financial sectors. To do this, the governments must invest more efficiently and use their scarce resources more effectively. An effective development partnership between the state and civil society would form the basis for private initiatives and encourage stakeholders to undertake a wider range of social and economic activities.

Size of Government. In the PMCs, government is larger than it is in almost all other comparable countries. Further, public expenditure as a proportion of GDP is unusually high. The results of large government have not been encouraging in promoting economic growth and development. The civil service is extensive, but has limited professional skills; budget and regulatory institutions and processes are inadequate, service levels are falling, and revenues are declining. In addition to providing core public services, PMC governments are involved in utilities, development finance, commercial credit, and overseas trade. Also, aid results have been ambiguous in the PMCs. An analysis of the relationship between total government expenditures, aid inflows, and GNP per capita reveals a strong correlation between high levels of total government expenditure and high levels of aid flows.

To compensate for skill shortages, agencies have taken to overstaffing with underqualified personnel, and governments have spent heavily on overseas training and have relied on outside technical assistance. The public sector commands most of the available resources and makes it difficult for the weak private sector to find and exploit new sources of growth.

Recent Policy Initiatives. Several countries are in the process of implementing Comprehensive Reform Programs (CRPs). The Federated States of Micronesia, the Marshall Islands, and Vanuatu have all been implementing wide-ranging economic policy and public sector reform programs with assistance from the Asian Development Bank (ADB). There are some countries, such as the Solomon Islands, where capacity to formulate program priorities and strategies and to develop multi-year public sector investment programs is weak.

The Report. This report discusses how the Pacific Islands development agenda could be put into practice, and it emphasizes three interlinking themes about enhancing the role of government:

- to focus on core functions; match the governments' tasks to their capacities, and to improve public sector accountability;

- to raise the efficiency of public sector spending through policies designed to quicken the pace of economic growth and reduce poverty; and

- to implement planning and budgetary procedures within the framework of a medium-term development horizon and to improve processes of public spending, including those programs financed through external aid.

Focusing on Core Functions of Government. Each PMC must select its core functions depending on its specific circumstances and vision of the future. However, there is convincing evidence that governments generally can best enhance economic and social welfare by concentrating on the following core functions:

- provide a stable macroeconomic environment that sets the right incentives for efficient economic activity;

- provide the institutional infrastructure, such as property rights, peace, law and order, and rules, to encourage efficient long-term investment;

- alleviate poverty by providing basic education, health care, and physical infrastructure; and

- protect the environment.

Governments' main tasks are to ensure that these core functions are in place. Activities should be fundamental to achieving economic development; and the government should be involved *only* if there are no efficient alternative providers. Basic education, health care, and physical infrastructure are the highest priorities to improve living standards for the widest group of poor people, and to lay the foundations for sustained, broad-based income growth. Public security, effective governance, non-distortionary economic policies, and sound environmental policies are also essential.

In the recent past, most PMC governments have maintained a generally prudent macroeconomic environment. However, fiscal slippages have begun to appear in some of the PMCs, and in combination with high inflation rates could threaten macroeconomic stability. Restoring fiscal balance through better public expenditure management and improved revenue collection is key. Of equal importance is the need to improve the incentive framework for stable and predictable tax and trade tariff regimes, market-oriented labor policies, and prudential regulation and governance arrangements for the financial sector. Steps in this direction have been already initiated, such as lowering import tariffs in some PMCs and actions to deal with the financial crisis of the National Bank of Fiji. But more needs to be done to improve the investment climate.

As regards to institutional infrastructure, the law and order situation in the PMCs fortunately presents no major problems for economic development. The main impediment seems to be access to land use within the customary land tenure system enshrined in the respective constitutions of the PMCs. The issue is not one of changing the land tenure system, but using land for productive purposes through better land-leasing mechanisms. With the exception of

Fiji, the PMCs have yet to develop institutional mechanisms for land leasing.

The PMCs have made much headway in building the social and physical infrastructure needed for development. Their focus should shift to improving preventive health, basic education, and asset maintenance, especially in infrastructure. Knowledge management and efficient use of information technologies to enhance traditional activities and generate new information-based activities have the potential for new economic opportunities.

Enhancing Private Sector Growth. Presently, the government markets agricultural goods and operates fishing fleets, mines, plantations, timber mills, aviation services, and hotels, plus engages in a wide range of other quasi-commercial activities. As a result, the private sector is constrained because it cannot compete with underpriced government services. Other serious impediments to private enterprise are limited access to land and credit, and cumbersome investment approval processes. PMC governments have begun to address some of these issues, but there is more to be done—such as establishing labor policies that are market-oriented and improving prudential supervision of the financial sector to prevent banking crises.

To Improve Governance, greater openness and public scrutiny of budgetary processes, public accounts, loan agreements, guarantees, public sector contracts, and audits are prerequisites. Governments must reduce tariffs and make them more uniform, eliminate exemptions and special treatment of selected industries, and minimize discretionary power. Foreign investment approval processes need to be transparent; and the judiciary and other regulatory bodies of government, such as the Ombudsman and Auditor General, strengthened.

Public Expenditure. PMCs suffer from two imbalances in the economic composition of expenditure: the first is between recurrent and investment expenditure, and the second is between the wage and non-wage components of recurrent expenditure. For example, in 1995, current expenditure exceeded 67 percent of total expenditure in most PMCs, and went up to 88 percent in Fiji. Most of this expenditure went to the government's own wage bill or supported the wage bill in other government entities.

The imbalance between operations and maintenance and other current expenditure is difficult to assess in the aggregate, but is likely to be high. Underprovisioning for operations and maintenance is a chronic problem that undermines development effectiveness in the Pacific Islands. The situation stands to be perpetuated when donors extend grant funds to replace or rehabilitate whatever has fallen apart for want of maintenance. Very often, the development budget is more sensitive to the availability of donor funds than it is to the exigencies of fiscal adjustment.

The optimal composition of government expenditure will differ in each country, depending on the activities and the relative costs of inputs. Evidence shows that high levels of current expenditure are a drag on growth, especially when an excessive share of current expenditure goes toward the wage bill or subsidies.

PMC governments are committed to improving the development effectiveness of expenditure, and they should carry out the reforms they have announced—streamlining government, public enterprises, and the civil service. This should be assisted by better planning, project preparation, and assessment and selection in the initial context of a medium-term public sector investment program (PSIP). The annual development budgets drawn from the PSIP should be derived from government policies and priorities, should be designed to complement and support government's current and planned service levels, and should be well integrated with the recurrent budget.

If government reduces the size of the civil service, the balance will improve between the wage bill, other current expenditure, and development expenditure. The civil service should move to more flexibility in its hiring practice, and adopt a performance-oriented remuneration system. A more cost-effective input combination should be reinforced by the performance/output budget systems which are now being put in place by some PMCs.

Improving Intrasectoral Expenditure, especially on health, education, and infrastructure, requires strong alignment with policies and priorities. In the health sector, government resources are concentrated on expensive curative and hospital services in urban areas, while preventive services and access to health care in rural areas are poor or non-existent. This is at odds with governments' policy to alleviate poverty. Greater participation by local community groups offers a cost-effective means of public health outreach. In the education sector, the challenge for most of the PMCs is to greatly improve the quantity and quality of education within budgetary constraints. The government should provide quality universal primary education using the most cost-effective input combination—possibly a mix of private and public education.

Despite the importance and scale of public investment in infrastructure, access to basic public services remains limited in most of the PMCs and service provision is low. Existing assets are not maintained and the allocations for operations are inadequate; departments and agencies are overstaffed and cost recovery is insufficient. Governments can improve the contribution of infrastructure to growth by managing the sector on commercial principles, and concentrating its resources in those areas with the highest social returns and large externalities. When it divests of infrastructure, it must create regulations to ensure that a public monopoly is not replaced by a private one. Such a replacement would merely restrict output and increase price and profits.

Planning and Budgeting. Well-functioning planning and budgetary systems are central to the performance of government and the achievement of economic reform goals. The budget and associated planning systems vary widely among the PMCs. Like most developing countries, the PMCs have relied upon a traditional, centralized budget system. But the emergence of fiscal deficits, and the realization that some traditional sources of funding may be disappearing, has led the PMC governments to examine how their budget systems can better support their development goals.

The traditional budget system has several advantages: it is straightforward, robust, and facilitates the control of spending. Nevertheless, there are many disadvantages, including a strong bias towards maintaining the *status quo.* The development effectiveness of public expenditure is hampered in the PMCs by the way the recurrent and development budgets have evolved and are separately prepared. Dual budgets emerged around the time of independence as a practical way of managing the growing volume of aid financing, and the political desire of governments to pursue a strategy of government-led development. The recurrent expenditure requirements of investments are not rigorously estimated when projects are prepared; this in turn, leads to inadequate provision for expenditures and unsustainable investments.

Furthermore, institutional responsibilities are typically divided, which exaggerates existing problems with prioritization and planning; projects are not integrated with the government's policies and priorities or the current budget. Governments lack the capacity for project preparation, and consequently, they rely on donors for technical assistance. This results in the development budget being largely driven by the donors' priorities.

A useful way of looking at a country's budget system is to assess its effectiveness at three levels. The first level is the capacity of the budget to articulate and fulfill the government's aggregate fiscal objectives. The second level of effective budgeting is the budget capacity to allocate resources based on strategic priorities. The third level, operational efficiency and effectiveness, is the budget's ability to support the delivery of programs and projects.

Traditional line-item budget systems can achieve operational efficiency and effectiveness if the country has a well-motivated public service, and if the budget is buttressed by departmental reporting and evaluation systems. Performance-oriented budget systems have a greater potential for operational efficiency, but need to be part of a broader set of incentives for good performance. Budget change alone will not achieve improved performance.

Performance-oriented reforms often require that the annual budget be prepared within a medium-term framework. A Medium-Term Expenditure Framework (MTEF) helps improve performance, particularly at the first two levels, but also, indirectly, at the third level. An MTEF can be an essential planning tool to help countries rein in the functions of government and ensure that resources are concentrated on priority programs. It makes the cost of policies transparent over time and enables programs to be compared with the available resources.

Performance-oriented budgets generally group closely related activities into programs to allow managers flexibility within the 'broad-band' of line items to manage their human and financial resources and achieve a specified outcome in the most cost-effective manner. However, a note of caution is in order. Devolving authority to lower levels to facilitate better use of resources *can work only if there is sufficient managerial capacity*. This has not been the case in many of the PMCs.

Full implementation of performance-oriented budgeting holds the potential to improve the productivity of public expenditure in the PMCs, but it is a complex undertaking. To be successful, both central and line agency managers must acquire resource management skills, and there must be major improvements in the cost accounting systems. If resource management is devolved *before* these conditions are met, productivity could decline. Performance-oriented budgeting also needs to be an integral part of a broader program of public management reform, which encourages a culture of performance. Changing budget rules alone will do little to improve performance, and may simply be disruptive. If government intends to outsource, staff capacity in procurement and contract management often requires strengthening.

The economies of the Pacific Islands are heavily dependent on foreign aid, which comprises a large proportion of their GDP. If not properly used and embedded in the country's own set of priorities, aid can be an impediment to sustainable growth. Donors are responding to this criticism and the ADB's current strategy for the Pacific suggests that any interventions must involve significant policy reform or capacity building and address key factors contributing to economic growth.

1. OVERVIEW

INTRODUCTION

Pacific Island governments are increasingly aware that state-led growth, based upon high levels of public investment and financed with aid flows, has not produced rapid increases in per capita incomes. Even though public investment has been substantial, growth has been disappointing. To make matters worse, the East Asian financial crisis appears to be pushing the islands into recession, underscoring the urgency of building a more resilient economic base. [1]

In response to these economic problems, governments have initiated strategies to improve the effectiveness of government activities. This report discusses how the Pacific Islands development agenda could be put into practice. It seeks to inform that agenda by analyzing the scope of government in the PMCs, their spending patterns and priorities, and finally, the budgetary processes that give rise to spending choices. The Action Plan issued at the Forum Economic Ministers' meeting emphasized strategies for economic reform that would strengthen government service delivery, improve the welfare of low-income groups, enhance the capacity of the private sector to generate sustained economic growth, and include greater consultation with community groups and the private sector. [2]

ECONOMIC PERFORMANCE

During the 1980s, the PMCs had invested an average of 29 percent of GDP in their economies, but economic growth remained stubbornly low at 2 percent a year. Investments were made in low-return projects, such as public buildings, or even in loss-making enterprises. In general, investments were managed ineffectively. State-led development has been disappointing in terms of sustainable economic growth, and in the PMCs, per capita real GDP growth has been much lower than in the Caribbean, African, and Indian Ocean islands (see figure 1.1).

The 1990s brought only a few improvements. The PMCs averaged a growth rate of 3.1 percent during 1992-96, although this is mainly due to Fiji which accounts for 62 percent of the total GDP of the PMCs. Growth was also nudged up by the major recovery in domestic production in Samoa after the cyclone devastations of 1990-92 (see table 1.1), and by unsustainable logging rates in the Solomon

---

[1] The nine Pacific Island Member Countries (PMCs) covered in this report are Fiji, Kiribati, Federated States of Micronesia, Marshall Islands, Palau, Samoa, Solomon Islands, Tonga and Vanuatu. The coverage in the main text excludes Palau which became a member in December 1997, but a separate country profile is presented in Annex 1.

[2] At the Forum Economic Ministers' meeting of July 1997, the five sessions covered were economic policy reform processes, institutional reform, investment policy, tariff policy, and multilateral trade agreements.

Islands. The PMCs' gross investment averaged 21 percent of GDP. Growth performance has been weak compared with islands outside the region. The Caribbean islands have enjoyed per capita GDP growth rates nearly twice that of the Pacific Islands, and even African islands have outperformed the Pacific Islands.

Figure 1.1: Average Growth Performance, 1985-95
(in percent per annum)

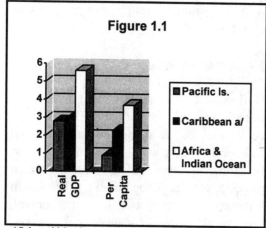

a/ Selected island economies
Source: World Bank

Despite a slight improvement in the productivity of investment during the 1990s[3], the overall marginal efficiency of investment remains low. The average incremental capital-output ratio (ICOR) is 7.2 for the PMCs as a whole, 12 percent less efficient than the average for all low-income countries[4] (Table 1.2). If Fiji is excluded, the remaining countries are less than 50 percent efficient. High ICORs or low returns to investment are associated with those PMCs that have larger shares of government expenditure. The implicit ICORs are highest in Kiribati, Tonga, Vanuatu, FSM, and the Marshall Islands and on the average, represent low returns to investment. These countries also have relatively high shares of government expenditure to GDP (see Chapter 3).

Table 1.1: GDP Growth, 1987-97
(in percent per annum)

	Average 1987-91	1992	1993	1994	1995	1996	Est. 1997	Average 1992-97
Fiji	2.4	4.9	2.2	3.9	2.1	3.1	-1.8	2.5
FSM	4.4	-1.2	5.7	1.4	1.0	1.0	-1.0	1.2
Kiribati	2.9	-1.6	1.0	1.7	3.3	1.9	3.0	1.6
Marshall Islands	4.4	0.1	4.1	2.8	3.7	-2.5	-10.0	-0.3
Solomon Islands	3.2	9.5	2.0	5.2	7.0	3.5	-1.0	4.4
Tonga	1.2	0.3	3.8	5.9	2.3	-0.4	-1.6	1.7
Vanuatu	2.8	-0.7	4.4	2.6	3.2	3.0	3.0	2.6
Samoa	-1.8	-0.2	4.1	-6.5	9.6	5.9	2.5	2.6
Average	2.4	3.7	2.8	3.3	3.0	2.7	-1.3	2.4

Source: World Bank Reports; IMF Recent Economic Development (various issues), ADB Report (April 1998).
Note: The above table does not reflect data which became available after May 1998.

---

[3] With the exception of Fiji, national accounts data remain poor in most PMCs.

[4] Excludes India and China.

Box 1.1: Pacific Islands - The Stylized Facts

The total land area of the PMCs, dispersed among hundreds of small islands and atolls, is only 63,802 square kilometers — equivalent to twice the size of Belgium. However, the total sea area controlled through exclusive economic zone (EEZ) agreements exceeds the land area of the United States of America or Canada. The total population of the PMCs is approximately 1.8 million, with Fiji accounting for 43 percent and the Marshall Islands accounting for only 3 percent of the total. The population growth rate has been relatively high, averaging 1.9 percent for the group.

The PMCs possess unique oceanographic features and agronomic and climatic conditions. Despite limited land mass, the natural resource base includes vast fisheries and other marine resources, forests, arable land and minerals. There is considerable tourism potential. Rich cultural traditions including the extended family system, customary land ownership, and benefit sharing practices have endowed their populations with a relatively safe and secure lifestyle. By world standards, the average life expectancy in the range of 60 to 70 years is favorable. However, the countries face formidable development challenges.

Like other small island economies, development is constrained by small internal markets, a narrow production base, high unit costs of infrastructure, and vulnerability to external shocks and natural disasters. Large external markets are far away, unlike the Caribbean islands that enjoy proximity to the large, high-income American markets, and the Indian Ocean island countries that are relatively close to the large European Union markets. The fragmented land mass and dispersed population frustrates transport and communications industries even among the small internal markets of each PMC.

The PMCs are quite diverse. They differ in ethnic composition from the Micronesian countries located in the North Pacific to the Polynesian and Melanesian countries located in the South Pacific. Their geographical terrain varies from atoll countries such as the Marshall Islands and Kiribati, to volcanic ones such as Vanuatu. The land and sea areas of the PMCs also differ considerably (see the table below). Fiji is the most developed country with a total GDP of US$2 billion. The distinctions between government workers and those in the non-government sector are not as clear-cut as they are in larger economies. Thus, public servants may also be employed in the private sector, or may be church or community leaders after working hours — an asset which could create greater synergy amongst the sectors.

Comparative Indicators

	Population ('000) 1995 (p.a.)	Population Growth Rate (1985-95)	Land Area (km2)	Sea Area ('000km2)	GDP 1995 (US$ mill.)	GNP Per Capita 1995 US$	Life Expectancy at Birth (years)a/	Infant Mortality ('000 births)
Pacific								
Fiji	790	1.07	18,272	1,146	1,999	2,440	72	21
FSM	107	2.21	705	2,500	216	2,010	63	32
Kiribati	80	1.97	810	3,550	48	920	58	55
Marshall Islands	56	3.99	181	1,942	103	1,670b/	61	63
Solomon Islands	375	3.19	27,990	1,500	327	910	63	41
Tonga	104	0.91	720	543	165	1,630	69	18
Vanuatu	169	2.72	12,190	680	238	1,200	64	41
Samoa	165	0.49	2,934	130	155	1,120	68	22

a/ 1992 or most recent estimate
b/ GDP per capita

Table 1.2: Marginal Efficiency of Investment

	GDP Growth % 1992-96	GDI % GDP 1992-96	Implicit ICOR
Fiji	2.7	15.3	5.6
FSM	1.6	22.0	13.8
Kiribati	1.3	26.5	20.4
Marshall Islands	2.4	32.1	13.8
Solomon Islands	6.0	31.0	5.2
Tonga	1.9	28.0	14.7
Vanuatu	2.5	35.0	14.0
Samoa	2.4	30.0	12.5
Weighted Average	2.9	21.0	7.2
Unweighted Average	2.6	27.5	12.5

Source: Data provided by the authorities and IMF Staff estimates.

THE EAST ASIAN FINANCIAL CRISIS

The East Asian financial crisis has begun to hurt the PMCs. Average economic growth rates appear to have turned sharply negative (table 1.1). Each country will be affected by the degree to which it has developed trade, investment, tourism, and aid linkages with the East Asian economies in crisis. There would also be secondary effects arising from the impact of the crisis upon Australia and New Zealand, the PMCs' traditional trading partners. The Solomon Islands will be deeply affected because of its strong and direct trade links with Japan and Korea. Fiji and Vanuatu are less influenced by direct links, but the indirect effects could be significant. In the other PMCs with relatively weak links with East Asian economies, the impact is small or negligible.[5]

In the Solomon Islands, the impact of the East Asian crisis arises from the collapse of the log export markets in Korea and Japan. Log exports had accounted for roughly half of export earnings and one third of government revenues in the mid-1990s. From a peak of 811,000 cubic meters of logging in 1996—three times the sustainable

yield—output has swung to almost zero production thus far in 1998. The export price has plummeted from about US$120 per cu. meter to less than US$65 per cu. meter—a price that the industry finds unprofitable to carry out logging, although they are still meeting some export orders from the stockpile. The real sector depends heavily on the multiplier effects of the logging industry such as transport and trading, feeder activities, and input supplies. In 1998, real GDP may decline by as much as 10 to 12 percent.

Relative to other PMCs, the Fiji economy is more diversified and, hence, potentially more resilient to external shocks; even so, the East Asian crisis has begun to take a severe toll. Tourist earnings have declined because there are fewer visitors and there has been a drop in potential investment. Secondary effects are likely to be more significant because Australia and New Zealand are Fiji's major trading partners and together they account for 40 percent of Fiji's merchandise exports. Consequently, Fiji's exports face a potential decline as the Asian crisis may result in slower growth in these countries, and as competition increases from Asian economies that have devalued their currencies. These changes combined with the effects of El Niño will likely result in a decline of real GDP of the order of 1 percent in 1998. In the case of Vanuatu, beef

---

[5] See Asian Development Bank, Impact of the Asian Financial Crisis on PMDC Economies, Final Report, April 1998.

exports to Papua New Guinea and Solomon Islands will drop, timber exports to Korea will decline, and tourist arrivals from Australia and New Zealand will diminish, but the overall loss to the economy is expected to be moderate. The North Pacific Islands are also likely to suffer from lower export prices for high grade fish to Japan and lower prices for copra and seaweed. However, the overall impact is likely to be small.

The full impact of the East Asian crisis upon the PMCs is not yet known, but the emerging situation underlines the need for the Pacific Islands to further diversify their production base and export markets and exercise greater prudential supervision over their respective financial sectors. In December 1997, the Solomon Islands devalued its currency to help restore competitive advantage, and in January 1998, Fiji did the same. The Solomon Islands has also embarked upon a major structural adjustment program, supported by both bilateral and multilateral financing institutions.

REKINDLING GROWTH

Establishing the conditions for recovery first, followed by more rapid sustained growth, will be essential to alleviate poverty. Although life is safe and secure in the Pacific Islands, the quality of life is deficient in some respects. For example, even in Fiji, with a per capita income of US$ 2,470 (1996), an estimated one in four people live below the poverty line. In Kiribati, life expectancy is low at 58 years, health and sanitation standards are extremely poor, the water is unsafe, and public health services are poor. In the Solomon Islands, malaria is endemic and is the chief cause of absenteeism in schools and the work place. Meanwhile, in Samoa there are indications of a social conflict between raised expectations of youth brought about by modernization forces, and blocked opportunities from obligations to a traditional society. Unless the Islands achieve moderate sustainable economic growth, further improvements in the quality of life may not be possible. Change is all the more essential because of vulnerability to external shocks and rising demands for modern goods and services, especially from the younger generations.

To rekindle economic growth, the PMCs must invest more efficiently. This, in turn, requires that the public sector use its scarce resources more effectively. Presently, the public share of total investment is high, but improvements to economic performance can only occur if these investments have a higher pay-off. In addition, government activities influence private performance through regulation, tariffs, and macro-policy; government activities also need to be more focused and strategic. Improving the efficiency of government expenditures would be facilitated by an effective development partnership between the state and the civil society. This would provide the private sector with incentives to save and invest in the productive sectors, and contribute to output and employment, while other stakeholders undertake a wider range of social and economic activities.

This report seeks to build upon the findings of previous Bank reports. The Pacific Islands report of 1995 discussed how the PMCs can enter the twenty-first century on a more resilient economic base. It suggested two broad approaches: first, to diversify the economic base into tourism and services; and second, to obtain higher returns from sustainable development and management of fisheries and forestry resources. The public expenditure reviews conducted in selected PMCs during 1996-97 examined ways in which the development effectiveness of public expenditure might be improved.

The report's *leitmotif* is structured broadly along three interlinked themes about "enhancing the role of government" by:

- focusing the government on core functions, matching its choice of tasks with its capacity, and improving public sector accountability;

- raising the efficiency of public sector spending through policies designed to quicken the pace of economic growth and reduce poverty; and

- implementing planning and budgetary procedures, within the framework of a medium-term development horizon, in order to improve processes of public spending, including those programs financed through external aid.

The above themes are closely interwoven (figure 1.2). While government focus on core functions will be essential to improve the organizational efficiency of service delivery, effective performance of these services will depend primarily on improved public resource allocation. In turn, effective public resource allocation will depend on improving the process of planning and budgeting within a medium-term framework.

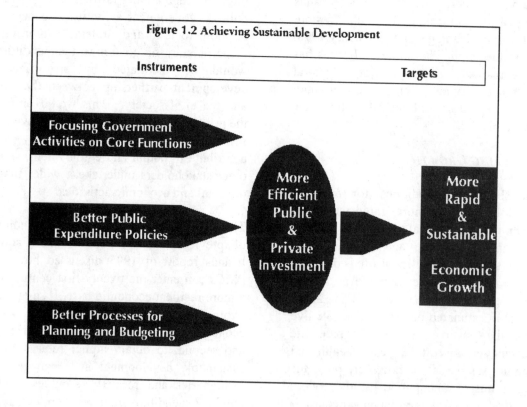

Figure 1.2 Achieving Sustainable Development

2. THE SCOPE OF GOVERNMENT: FOCUSING ON ESSENTIAL PUBLIC ACTIVITIES

STRUCTURE AND SIZE OF GOVERNMENT

In most of the Pacific Island Member Countries, government is larger than virtually all other countries at similar stages of development. Public expenditures constitute an unusually large share of GDP. The civil service is large, but has limited skills; budget and regulatory institutions and processes are weak; service levels are declining; and revenues become more difficult to raise. In most of the PMCs, the private sector is small, or functions poorly.

Consequently, government has expanded and, over the years, supported by generous infusions of foreign aid, activities broadened to include public enterprises engaged in production, marketing, and trading. As government grew, it failed to create many new opportunities for the private sector. Through lack of alternatives, government has become the 'default' employer of skilled and educated workers. Today this swollen public sector is in acute danger of sinking under its own weight.

Chart 2.1: Government Expenditure in Low and Middle Income Economies [a]

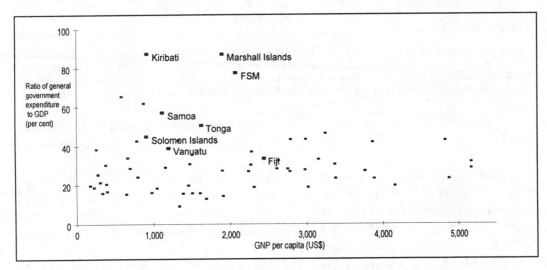

a   The ratio of expenditure to GDP for the PMCs is for either 1995 or 1996 (as outlined in Annex 3), the ratio for Caribbean countries is an estimate for 1994, and the ratio for other developing countries is for 1995. The estimates of GNP per capita are for 1995 and are derived using the Altlas method (except for the FSM and the Marshall Islands which are GDP per capita in 1994).

Sources: Annex 1, World Bank 1997a, World Bank 1996a, AusAID 1997.

Today, the PMC governments are engaged in a wide range of economic activities, such as utilities, development finance, commercial credit, and overseas trade. They market agricultural goods and operate fishing fleets, mines, plantations, timber mills, aviation services, hotels, and a wide

servants than the eight PMCs. Not surprisingly, aid flows, which finance both recurrent and development expenditure, also contributed to the size of government. The relationship of total government expenditures with aid inflows and GNP per capita was analyzed and the results show a

Chart 2.2: The Government Wage and Salary Bill in Low and Middle Income Economies [a]

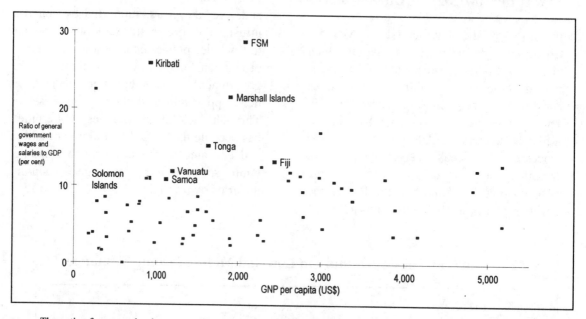

a   The ratio of wage and salary expenditure to GDP for the PMCs is for either 1995 or 1996 (as outlined in Annex 3), the ratio
        for Caribbean countries is for either 1993 or 1994 (except for Trinidad and Tobago which is 1992), and the ratio for other
        developing countries is based on the average for 1991 to 1995. The estimates of GNP per capita are for 1995 and are
        derived using the Atlas method (except for the FSM and the Marshall Islands which are GDP per capita in 1994).

range of other quasi-commercial activities (see Annex 3).

Chart 2.1 presents the ratio of general government expenditure to GDP for 62 low and middle income countries for which data are available. With the exception of Fiji, the ratios for PMCs are much above average, and Kiribati, the Marshall Islands, and FSM "lead" the group. The picture is even more startling when considering the level of government wages and salaries as a share of GDP for the same 62 countries. As shown in Chart 2.2, few countries allocate significantly more of GDP to paying civil

strong correlation between total government expenditure and aid flows (see Annex 6).

Based on this analysis, table 2.1 below shows the average predicted value of government spending associated with a particular level of aid and GNP per capita.

The range of activities carried out by government is wide, considering the shortages of technical and managerial resources. As a result, limited skills are spread too thinly resulting in sub-standard performance. Governments have responded to this situation by overstaffing agencies with partially-qualified personnel, spending heavily on overseas training, and relying on outside technical assistance to fill gaps. In some services, technical assistance has become an almost permanent feature of government. Meanwhile, the few qualified public servants tend to be heavily over-burdened, and this is not sustainable.

business. The objective is to suggest ways of reducing the scope of government intervention while supporting private activities. It concludes with a discussion of ways to improve governance and public

Table 2.1: As Aid Flows Increase So Does Government Expenditure

	GNP per Capita (US dollars)						
	700	1000	1300	1600	1900	2200	2500
Grants/GDP (%)	Total Expenditure/GDP						
10	55.3	51.4	47.5	43.6	39.7	35.8	31.9
20	68.1	64.2	60.3	56.4	52.5	48.6	44.7
30	80.9	77.0	73.1	69.2	65.3	61.4	57.5
40	93.7	89.8	85.9	82.0	78.1	74.2	70.3
50	106.5	102.6	98.7	94.8	90.9	87.0	83.1

Source: Annex 6, Equation 1.

PMC governments also recognize the dilemma of a dominant public sector and a thin, under-developed private sector. Governments are increasingly aware that the private sector and other stakeholders should play a greater role in achieving sustainable economic growth and development, but it is the public sector that has access to the financial and technical resources needed to undertake complex tasks. It is difficult for the private sector to find and exploit new sources of growth when the public sector has already established footholds in the key commercial segments of the economy.

The governments of the region influence their economies through several channels: macroeconomic policy, regulation, allocation of capital through the financial system, and public spending. This chapter, after reviewing recent reform initiatives, examines recent macroeconomic policies and selected regulatory policies affecting

accountability. The next chapter analyzes public expenditures.

RECENT POLICY INITIATIVES TO REFORM THE PUBLIC SECTOR

Fiji has an impressive array of frameworks and principles and was successful in developing and implementing a broad-ranging reform program for several years following the 1987 military coups. Fiji implemented a policy package focused on making the economy more outward oriented, more in tune with market forces, and less dependent on government. Significant progress was made in reducing protection against imports and an ambitious program of privatization and corporatization was undertaken. The Government also amended labor laws to help make labor markets more flexible and introduced a value added tax (VAT). However, Fiji has made limited progress in reducing the size of government.

In 1993, the Fiji Government outlined its policies and strategies in *Opportunities for Growth*. Many of the priorities in that document remain relevant to Fiji. A recent report on strategic planning prepared for the Fiji Government argued for a central role for government in terms of three core functions. Key features of the report were that Fiji should develop an enabling legal framework, sound market-oriented economic policies, strong human resources, carefully appraised public investment programs, and better access by the economically weak to opportunities and social services.

In the 1997 and 1998 Fiji budgets, priority has been given to primary and secondary education, preventive health, roads and bridges, and agricultural development. The emphasis on basic education, preventive health, and infrastructure in support of private sector development fits well with core functions. Agricultural development is considered in more detail later in this chapter.

The Fiji government is trying to ensure that there is maximum cooperation and coordination among ministries, that collective decisions are based on sound analysis, that scarce technical resources are better utilized, and that there is a more transparent policymaking process with participation from the private sector and Non-Government Organizations (NGOs). Four consultative committees have been established: economic policies; fiscal policies and public sector reform; human resource development and social policies; and the primary sector and infrastructure. The committees will include NGOs, unions, business groups, and the council of chiefs. Fiji has also established regional planning

units to work closely with community groups in the development process. Planning units in the Ministries of Education, Health, Agriculture, Forestry and Fisheries, and Public Works are also being strengthened. This should help clarify the role of government at the sectoral level established for economic policies, fiscal policies and public sector reform, and human resource development. Several countries are in the process of implementing Comprehensive Reform Programs (CRPs). The Federated States of Micronesia, the Marshall Islands and Vanuatu have all been implementing wide ranging economic policy and public sector reform programs with assistance from the ADB.

The program in Vanuatu is very ambitious: it identifies over 120 activities and some 50 legislative reform items. The CRP has been underway since early 1997. It features renewing the institutions of governance, redefining a role for the public sector, improving public sector efficiency, encouraging private sector led growth, and improving equity (ADB 1997c). Good governance is considered a prerequisite to all the reforms. Important proposals include clarifying legally the roles of ministers, their political advisers and the public service; improving parliamentary procedures; enhancing the capacity and independence of the judiciary; removing political interference; and developing a performance-oriented culture. The role of the public sector is being redefined to avoid government involvement in commercial activities. Important objectives are to establish a stable, non-distortionary, business-friendly environment and to devote more resources to education and to provide and maintain infrastructure.

The Vanuatu CRP was formulated through an extensive nation-wide consultative and participatory process. To maintain continued ownership of the program and ensure effective implementation, it will be important to continue consultation and participation from all sectors of the community.

In some countries, capacity is weak both to formulate program priorities and strategies and to develop multi-year public sector investment programs. The Solomon Islands has been experiencing a fiscal crisis for the previous several years, exacerbated now by the East Asian financial crisis. It is developing a structural reform program under a new coalition government of five political groups. Many of the problems in the Solomon Islands result from poor governance outcomes. Formal institutions for good governance have existed for a long time, but many of these seem to be readily bypassed and independent enforcement does not occur.

The Solomon Islands reform program has established two task forces to focus on economic reform and public sector reform (Solomon Islands Government 1997). The economic reform component recognizes that the highest priority must be given to fiscal stability. In relation to structural policies, the priority issues include trade and investment liberalization. The framework document recognizes that the reform program will require "ownership" by the people and that wide ranging and regular consultation and briefings are needed. The intentions and approach expressed in the framework document are similar to features of the Vanuatu CRP.

In terms of equity, the policies and actions of PMC governments reconfirm their commitment to assist disadvantaged groups and isolated communities. The provision of basic education and health services and subsidized transport are common means of assisting isolated communities. Governments also have the responsibility for helping people who are made redundant as a result of public sector reforms to find new opportunities in the private sector.

FOCUSING ON CORE FUNCTIONS OF GOVERNMENT

Of course, it is the prerogative of each PMC to define its core functions as these depend on specific country circumstances and a vision of the future. But as a general rule, governments can best enhance economic and social welfare by concentrating on the following fundamental, or core functions:

- provision of a stable macroeconomic environment that sets the right incentives for efficient economic activity;

- provision of an institutional infrastructure, such as property rights, peace, law and order, and rules, to encourage efficient long-term investment;

- alleviation of poverty by providing basic education, health care, and economically viable physical infrastructure required for economic activity; and

- protection of the environment.

Two criteria are helpful when considering whether an activity is a core function. First, it must be determined whether the activity is fundamental to achieving economic development. And second, it must be determined whether it is likely that the activity will not be provided or will be underprovided if the government does not provide or coordinate it. The government itself does not have to undertake all core functions, but it should ensure that they take place.

These core functions are directly relevant not only for supporting market-oriented activity. Basic education, health care, and physical infrastructure are the highest priority to improve living standards for the widest group of poor people, as well as lay the foundations for sustained, broad-based income growth. (Public expenditures for these are discussed in the next chapter). Public security, effective governance, non-distortionary economic policies, and sound environmental policies are also essential to directly improve the welfare of the poor. The key task is to ensure that fundamental or core functions are in place. Once this has been achieved, more attention can be focused on a range of other specific economic and social problems.

STABLE, CREDIBLE, AND NON-DISTORTIONARY ECONOMIC POLICIES

MACROECONOMIC STABILITY. Ensuring a stable macroeconomic regime and a consistent, non-distortionary approach to all

situation has worsened in 1995-96. At the same time, the PMCs recorded an average inflation rate of 5.4 percent during 1992-96 (see Annex 1 for country-specific inflation rates), which was double the world inflation rate during the same period. The overall effect has been a weakening of the respective currencies. The combined effect of fiscal slippage and high inflation rates is the risk of macroeconomic instability, which the PMC governments need to address.

Experience has shown that large and persistent fiscal deficits that are financed through seigniorage lead to macroeconomic instability and that high government current expenditure is not conducive to economic growth. This is because macroeconomic stability is a precondition for private entrepreneurs to produce goods for domestic and external markets at predictable costs and

Table 2.2: PMC Government Resources, Expenditure, Deficits and Growth
(In percent of GDP)

	Av. Govt. Expenditure 1985-89	Av. Govt. Expenditure 1990-95	Av. Govt. Revenue 1990-95	Av. External Grants, 1990-95	Av. Govt. Balance incl. Grants 1990-95
Kiribati	84.6	100.6	79.4	39.3	17.8
Marshall Islands 1/	62.1	98.1	31.8	55.2	-11.9
FSM 1/	83.0	89.8	29.7	59.7	-2.0
Samoa 1/	52.5	70.1	41.8	13.4	-11.8
Solomon Islands	38.7	53.1	28.9	14.6	-7.4
Tonga 1/	45.8	43.4	26.3	14.6	-3.8
Vanuatu	53.9	39.4	23.8	14.6	-3.5
Fiji	28.0	28.4	26.5	0.3	-1.6

Source: World Bank Regional Economic Reports, Public Expenditure Reviews and Country Economic Memoranda; IMF Staff Reports and Recent Economic Developments.
1/ Fiscal year data are recorded in the calendar year in which the fiscal year ends.

economic policies is one of the core functions of government. Most PMCs have espoused such policies, but practices and outcomes vary from the ideal standard. Several PMCs have had a budgetary crisis. Large fiscal deficits are a problem in Fiji, the Federated States of Micronesia, the Marshall Islands and the Solomon Islands (tables 2.2 to 2.4). Moreover, the fiscal

at the required quality. In some cases, such as the Cook Islands, Federated States of Micronesia, and the Marshall Islands, difficult decisions have been taken to reduce public expenditure; the Solomon Islands is developing proposals for a structural adjustment program. Privatization and various forms of commercialization are also underway in most PMCs, although progress

Table 2.3: Government Overall Balance, including Grants
(In percent of GDP)

	Av. 85-89	1990	1991	1992	1993	1994	1995	1996
Fiji	-3.1	0.3	-1.4	-3.0	-3.4	-1.5	-0.5	-4.7
Kiribati	-1.5	-7.2	-1.4	34.2	43.1	24.6	13.2	-7.2
FSM	16.8	3.8	-8.0	-5.3	-3.3	-0.6	1.6	-
Marshall Islands	7.0	1.8	-6.8	-26.3	-14.0	-13.5	-12.5	-
Samoa	3.3	-1.1	-9.9	-16.5	-22.0	-11.5	-9.6	1.9
Solomon Islands	-7.7	-6.9	-13.3	-7.2	-7.9	-6.6	-2.4	-4.0
Tonga	-0.6	-7.3	-10.1	-6.6	1.8	2.5	-3.2	-3.9
Vanuatu	-2.3	-10.1	-1.6	-3.3	-1.4	-3.0	-1.6	-

Source: Statistical Appendix on Public Finance.

Table 2.4: Public Debt Indicators, 1995-96

	Government Debt (in % of GDP)	External Debt Service (in % of Exports of Goods and Services)	Expenditure on Interest (in % of Current Government Expenditure)
Fiji	40.6 [2/]	4.7 [1/]	12.0 [2/]
Kiribati	13.2 [5/]	0.2	0.3
FSM	55.4 [4/]	18.3 [4/]	3.6
Marshall Islands	118.2 [3/]	43.8	10.1
Samoa	95.2 [3/]	9.6	3.6
Solomon Islands	61.5 [1/]	9.7 [2/]	13.9
Tonga	45.9	16.2	...
Vanuatu	18.7 [3/]	0.6 [1/]	2.6

Source: World Bank Regional Economic Reports, Public Expenditure Reviews and Country Economic Memoranda; IMF Staff Reports and Recent Economic Developments.

1/ As of end of 1995. 2/ Actual 1996. 3/ External public debt only as of 1996. 4/ External debt only, as of the end of 1994/95. 5/ External debt only, as of 1996.

has generally been slow. If all PMCs are to secure a better economic future, they must commit to sustaining a disciplined fiscal approach, reducing government current expenditure, and reducing government involvement in commercial activities.

TARIFFS. To encourage investment that will contribute the maximum to the economy, governments must develop and implement policies that use economic resources efficiently. Most PMCs have relatively high tariffs, ranging from effective nominal *ad*

valorem rates of 10 to 40 percent. These tariffs have had protective effects for some import-competing activities and have raised the cost structure of the economy, consequently, reducing the competitiveness of exports. However, in many PMCs the effects of other factors such as locational disadvantages, high reservation wages, a high real exchange rate underwritten by generous aid, remittances, and in some cases, resource rents, may well have been more important constraints on international competitiveness. An exception has been Fiji where a sizable import-competing sector developed behind the protective effect of high tariffs. Tariffs have since been reduced substantially, helping to create a more efficient manufacturing sector. However, the sugar, clothing, and tuna industries in Fiji; the motor vehicle harness wiring factory in Samoa; and the tuna industry in the Solomon Islands have relied heavily on preferential access to developed country markets and their risk is that their long-term security is not underwritten by a fundamental comparative advantage.

FOREIGN INVESTMENT. The main protective policy in the PMCs relates to restrictions on foreign investment and foreign business activities. There are still important institutional and policy impediments such as access to land or lengthy approval processes to a healthy flow of foreign investment. The private sector of most PMCs is weak or dominated and constrained by the size and role of the public sector. Yet most people wish to improve their standard of living through better opportunities in the cash economy. This suggests that governments should help establish conditions to attract more foreign investment to PMCs. Greater foreign involvement and direct investment in PMCs would be the best way of upgrading and integrating PMC economies into world markets (ADB 1997b). Governments could help remove all formal barriers to foreign investment and could establish conditions and institutions that clearly define and protect property rights.

Policy credibility is essential to foster the private sector confidence required to develop the investment and financial sectors. Recently, the fiscal crisis in the Solomon Islands caused the government to renege on interest obligations. This will dampen the future willingness of private financial institutions to hold government bonds and will increase risk premiums on all

lending in the Solomon Islands. In most PMCs, including Fiji, the private sector is disturbed by the lack of an investor-friendly policy climate.

LAW AND PROPERTY RIGHTS

Effective property rights have three basic characteristics: public security and protection from theft; protection from arbitrary government actions, ranging from unexpected and *ad hoc* changes in regulations and taxes to outright corruption; and a fair, independent and predictable judiciary. A fully efficient property rights system requires additional demanding conditions that involve complete and exclusive specification and effective enforcement of all entitlements and no restrictions on transferability of property rights to others.

A common feature of PMCs is the tradition of customary forms of land ownership and kinship traditions of sharing resources. Traditional land tenure ensures that all family and clan members have access to land; strong kinship bonds and customs encourage traditional sharing of economic wealth. This tradition of sharing also serves to validate rights to common property. In some cases customary legal systems still coexist with formal legal systems. Customary legal systems allocate rights according to status in society, roles, age, and gender. In contrast, the modern cash economy entails a legal system that recognizes individual rights, gender equality, and individual ownership of property.

The above arrangements have served PMCs well to avoid absolute poverty and they are an informal social security mechanism. However, they also constrain market-based activity by reducing the incentive to work hard, save and engage in entrepreneurial activity. Cultural preservation is an important value in the PMCs and most governments are keen to support it. The key issue is not one of changing the land tenure system *per se*, but of unlocking land tied up in unproductive uses because of inflexible rules governing its ownership and use. This involves improving land leasing mechanisms through greater community participation (see also Annex 4).

Land issues in the PMCs present a major challenge for development. In Fiji, 83 percent of land is owned by indigenous Fijians and cannot be bought or sold. In Samoa, 84 percent of the land area is held under customary ownership and cannot be bought or sold except to the government for public purposes. A limited amount of freehold land can only be bought or sold by Samoan citizens. In Kiribati, land can be bought and sold by I-Kiribati but only with the approval of the Land Court. In Vanuatu, almost all land is under custom except for public land in Port Vila and Luganville. Long-term leases can be obtained, but these are vulnerable to challenge and renegotiation. Very little land has been formally registered in the Solomon Islands and Vanuatu, and registration is far from complete in Micronesia. Freehold land cannot be bought or sold in the Cook Islands, Federated States of Micronesia, Tonga and Tuvalu. Generally, customary land is more important in rural communities, while formal law usually dominates land under intense use (ADB 1996b, 1997b). Customary systems of land tenure do not provide formal ownership but a system of access to land, often involving multiple use. All land rights are in a constant but slow process of renegotiation according to the relative needs and powers of various individuals and groups.

Development of customary land is sometimes frustrated by numerous disputes over ownership. Once land is leased, customary owners can often unilaterally reopen negotiations if they consider the leaseholder is doing well. Land held under customary tenure cannot normally be collateralised for securing a loan. This retards investment and the development of a capital market. For foreign investors, lack of security of tenure is the major constraint to investment, especially large-scale investment. Secure tenure requires that rights are clearly specified and enforced. There are numerous examples of attacks and threats on tourist resorts that highlight the problem.[1]

In this respect, there may be scope for selective reforms or arrangements that facilitate access to land where there is substantial demand for economic use. Effective administrative arrangements can be developed by the government to provide a sound leasing system and effective mechanisms to resolve disputes. Governments must also develop more secure property rights for foreign investors. One option that may be worth considering is some form of regional insurance or multilateral investment guarantee arrangements to protect foreign investors from breaches of leases, attacks, damage and seizure of their assets.

In Fiji there are major problems with the expiry and renewal of sugar land leases. There are 5,345 leases due to expire in 1997-2005, and 3,384 in 2000-2001. Native Land Trust Board (NLTB) surveys clearly indicated that most landowners want the land back to grow sugar themselves. If this happens many Fiji-Indians will be displaced. The NLTB is developing proposals for more flexible leases, including rolling leases over from 5 to 30 years.

---

[1] Relevant examples are the incidents at Anuha resort in Solomon Islands, the resorts off Lautoka in Fiji, and at Mulifanaua resort in Samoa.

In Fiji, constitutional uncertainty has also contributed to lack of investor confidence (Economic Insights 1995). Although this has been formally addressed, there are still reservations about the effectiveness of the constitution and the government's ability to ease cultural tensions. If the government can resolve the sugar land lease problem, it would improve investor perceptions of the political and constitutional environment.

ENHANCING PRIVATE SECTOR GROWTH: A SUPPORTIVE ROLE FOR GOVERNMENT IN KEY AREAS

LABOR MARKETS. The main labor market issues in PMCs relate to the underemployment of labor in the economy as a whole, and the unproductive use of labor in the public sector. A focus on basic education and health care will improve the supply side of the labor market, but job growth will depend on the extent to which the government is able to foster private development. Policies that focus on undertaking the core functions of government and attracting significant foreign investment offer the best prospects. Governments also need to ensure that labor markets are flexible and that firms have the ability to hire and dismiss or reallocate workers easily and that pay is determined by market forces. Reforms to reduce the involvement of government in commercial activities and ensure that pay reflects performance are critical.[2]

AGRICULTURE. Governments can improve the agricultural sector performance through many activities. Applied research to improve yields and identify new varieties and extension services to disseminate information about new varieties, technology transfer and implementing quarantine

requirements are cases in point for government. They are justified because of excessive transactions costs and lack of property rights for individuals. Generally, marketing is best left to the private sector, but there can be a role for a commercially oriented government organization which could help small holders to sell their goods in large markets so they could overcome transactions costs and avoid market power problems. It is important to ensure that the quality of agricultural products is adequate, particularly for exports. Rather than undertake this function, government should ensure that such a system is in place; for example, by empowering industry associations to set and enforce quality standards (see World Bank RER 1993).

Many of the PMC governments undertake these functions but with varying degrees of success depending on focus and capability. Often PMCs extend themselves unnecessarily and get directly involved in commercial production and marketing. Recent experiences in Fiji highlight the issue. The Government did not consider agricultural development to be a priority in the 1997 budget in Fiji, but subsequently developed an initiative known as the Commodity Development Framework (CDF). The CDF includes a range of functions. It includes core functions such as providing infrastructure, plus other functions that aim to address market failures. The CDF may have many valuable aspects but there is no convincing, analytical or empirical rationale for the government to be directly involved in production and commercial investment in agriculture in Fiji.

FORESTRY. There is an important role for government in the forestry sector because property rights are poorly defined, there are adverse environmental externalities, and a weak information system. Forest resources need to be managed to take appropriate account of current and future generations.

---

[2] For a detailed discussion, see Asian Development Bank, Domestic Resource Mobilization and Economic Growth in the PDMCS, 1997.

Governments must make appropriate institutional arrangements so that royalties and tax revenues are adequately collected, felling and regeneration practices are undertaken, and landowners understand their rights, responsibilities and options with respect to logging. In the Solomon Islands, a main concern is that extraction rates have been highly excessive, which may reflect *ad hoc* approaches to issuing licenses, the domination of powerful interest groups and weak enforcement capacity. Many of the problems relate to wider governance issues that can only be addressed with significant political commitment and capability (see World Bank RER 1995).

FISHERIES. Direct government involvement in the fisheries sector has not been successful in the PMCs. This is an area where private sector-led development would be more beneficial to the countries, given the kind of flexibility in operations required. The government's role should be to develop and enforce conservation policy, to collect and disseminate information on fish resources and harvests, to negotiate and enforce access fees for foreign vessels and to encourage shore-based fishing activities. Experience elsewhere has shown that it is best to avoid direct equity investments or direct involvement in production and marketing (see World Bank RER 1995).

INDUSTRY. The development of industry in PMCs is generally difficult and slow. Often the government has reached beyond its capacity in attempting to develop industry and business. The most effective approach is to ensure that the basic requirements of secure property rights, non-distortionary and stable economic policies, and basic infrastructure are in place. More specific interventions, such as supporting business by providing information, advice and training, can be beneficial if they are provided on an equal opportunity basis and focused on the basic business needs.

Experience has shown that policies with significant discretionary components run the risk of corruption and inefficient investment.[3]

TOURISM. Hitherto, tourism growth in the PMCs has fallen short of the rate for Asia and the Pacific Region as a whole. This sector has considerable potential to contribute to broad-based economic development and to generate many jobs. The key is to encourage large-scale foreign investment. Where there is market potential, foreign investors' main problems are access to land, enforcement of contracts, freedom to repatriate capital and selling ownership rights. Other important considerations are the freedom to use foreign labor and the low costs of bureaucratic procedures. The situation in Vanuatu highlights the issue. To realize its potential as a tourist destination, it needs large-scale investment in resorts and infrastructure. Although governments have recognized the need for substantial investment they are ambivalent about foreign investment and, therefore, demonstrate a marked reluctance to change foreign investment policy (see World Bank RER 1995, ADB 1996b).

PUBLIC ENTERPRISES. Many countries have developed commercialization and privatization programs, but progress has been slow. The efficiency of the public enterprise sector is an important determinant of business competitiveness through its role in supplying infrastructure inputs and a range of goods and services. Effective privatization is difficult to achieve in PMCs. This reflects a lack of understanding of the benefits of private incentives in a

---

3 See Foreign Investment Advisory Service, Pacific Island Country Foreign Policies: A Further Assessment of Transparency, a Background paper at the FEMM, July 1997. See also, South Pacific Forum Secretariat, Foreign Investment Climate in South Pacific Forum Countries, August 1995.

competitive environment, weak business and entrepreneurial skills and motivation, slow economic growth, small domestic capital markets and resistance to foreign ownership. When public ownership is retained, attempts at corporatization have generally focused on changing the legal status of entities, paying insufficient attention to issues such as setting clear and non-conflicting objectives and establishing effective accountability systems. Fiji has developed a state-of-the-art public enterprise policy framework and is planning to review and develop a more appropriate competition framework for all economic activities. However, lack of resources to manage the reforms is a key problem. The workload on the public sector would diminish greatly over time if significant privatization could be achieved. The development of adjustment packages to manage the transition for displaced workers and a willingness to facilitate more foreign investment are crucial for making real progress. Also, in the case of public utilities, privatization needs to be accompanied by an effective regulatory framework to ensure pricing, coverage and quality issues are adequately covered.

FINANCIAL MARKETS. Various market failures emanating from information problems can lead to gaps in credit availability and a significant risk of instability in the solvency of the financial system. However, government must ensure that any intervention to address such problems is effective and provides a net benefit to society. Effective governance arrangements for government-owned financial institutions is particularly important. The failure of the National Bank of Fiji highlights this problem (World Bank RER 1993).

ENVIRONMENT. Governments are best suited to dealing with environmental problems through licensing or approval systems and monitoring to ensure environmental standards are met. In the PMCs, the major environmental problems tend to be caused by land clearing for agriculture, in-shore fishing or waste disposal. The solutions to these problems often rest with the local community and the role of governments is to educate the community to improve their own environmental management. Governments also provide the physical infrastructure required for waste management and the institutions required to oversee high risk commercial activities such as logging, and monitor environmental conditions (see Annex 4 and World Bank RER 1993).

TELECOMMUNICATIONS AND KNOWLEDGE MANAGEMENT. Access to relevant information and knowledge is essential to integrate the Pacific Islands into the global economy. In the twenty-first century, the global market will be linked electronically, and commodities will be cheap and trade will be global. Even now, trends in international competitiveness clearly indicate how knowledge and information contribute to enhance the value added in traditional activities such as agriculture, small-scale manufacturing and tourism. They generate new production and support opportunities based on activities such as data entry, remote secretarial services, engineering design, and trade facilitation. In addition, using information technologies effectively will be crucial to rapidly improve the delivery of educational services, training and health services, and other government services. More importantly, the PMCs need to position themselves for niche markets in new information-based industries which will be the engines of wealth and prosperity into the next century.[4]

Some initiatives have already been made; for example, Fiji is considering improving

---

[4] See also Michio Kaku, "Visions: How Science will Revolutionize the 21st Century," 1997.

telecommunications infrastructure or developing new information applications. A systematic analysis was recently undertaken of how effectively Pacific Island countries are exploiting the potential of the information revolution and what specific policy measures countries should consider to boost their competitiveness by using knowledge and information. The analysis indicated that the main strengths the PMCs could build upon are their small and manageable populations, generally high literacy and significant international links and their location between major markets in the Pacific rim. But the chief constraints are: (a) shortcomings of investment and expenditure on telecommunications infrastructure, weak arrangements for collecting and structuring information to enhance economic opportunities and participation; (b) low level of computer use and the high cost of Internet access and lack of financial resources; and (c) lack of a national vision and strategy for promoting improved access to and use of the information and knowledge throughout these economies and societies.

Inter-country experience suggests information-intensive industries and related investments will flow into centers of efficiency which are largely characterized by up-to-date infrastructure and trained personnel. In this regard, PMC policy makers need to focus on the following inter-related layers of the knowledge economy for policy development and activity flows:

- to improve telecommunications and Internet access for generating, trans-mitting, and retrieving information, and thereby, improve service delivery through greater sharing of information across agencies;

- to identify data which could be used for production purposes by the public and private sectors, and help establish a stronger public-private relationship; to

ensure availability of trained personnel, institutions and processes involved in the generating, dissemination and use of information; and

- to identify and foster applications to a wide range of economic and social activities.[5]

IMPROVING GOVERNANCE: REDUCING ADMINISTRATIVE DISCRETION AND IMPROVING PUBLIC ACCOUNTABILITY

At its broadest level, governance refers to the authority, control and management functions of government, and mechanisms to ensure the accountability of government and its officials. While the power of the state affords the flexibility to contribute to economic development, it also carries the risks of arbitrary behavior that could constrain economic and social welfare. Box 2.1 outlines some key governance principles for most formal democratic situations.

Effective government intervention must be motivated by a broadly agreed set of goals that seek to improve overall welfare. However, often government intervention may help special interest groups that are lobbying for special incentives and preferences. If capacity is limited, discretionary powers can result in an *ad hoc* approach to policy and regulations or possible corruption, which severely damages growth and development. In the Pacific Islands, there are two more complicating factors. First, in many small Pacific societies, applying sanctions to individuals who underperform runs against societal norms and this can significantly weaken public accountability. Second, accountability through formal democratic

---

5 See World Bank, Pacific Islands Knowledge Assessment (1998/99), based on reports by SMEC International Pty. Ltd. Insearch Ltd., University of Technology, Sydney and Carl Bro a/s, Informatics.

institutions is weakened by the lack of public information about the performance of their elected officials.

Corruption is not endemic in the Pacific Islands, but there have been problems in some countries. Officials have been vulnerable to "get-rich-quick" operators. There have been scams that have involved the loss of public funds and there have been allegations of corruption. Other forms of governance failure arise in customs, logging activities, foreign investment approval, tendering procedures, government-owned banks and public pension funds. In some cases, it is not corruption, but poor guidelines, weak management and inadequate skills that preclude good governance. In other cases, cultural factors can facilitate the acceptance of corrupt behavior of political leaders.

Addressing the above requires introducing policies and establishing mechanisms that reduce or eliminate the scope for monopoly-type power and discretionary behavior at the political and administrative level, and create an appropriate balance between accountability and flexibility.[6] An economic policy regime that minimizes distortions and exemptions will reduce the scope for officials to favor particular individuals or firms. There should be low, relatively uniform tariffs, and minimal specific industry assistance; exclusive licenses should be avoided. Reforms to enhance political, administrative and economic competition can also be helpful. However, privatization and commercialization processes can also bring

opportunities for corruption. Tendering procedures should be open and truly competitive; there should be transparent and reliable regulatory and performance monitoring to support privatization and commercialization. Also, there should be processes to promote transparency and ensure accountability, credible law enforcement, and an effective judiciary.

Most Pacific Island countries have developed measures to counteract corruption and improve governance. The formal system of governance and accountability is reflected in a range of legislation including the constitution, public finance and audit acts, standing orders of parliament, financial regulations, public service regulations and other formal arrangements.

Accountability measures continue to be improved. Several countries now have leadership codes in place. In response to serious financial difficulties, the Cook Islands has demonstrated a strong, commitment to government transparency and accountability. In particular, it has adopted a fiscal responsibility system along the lines of that in place in New Zealand. This will help ensure public scrutiny of economic and fiscal information and plans. Several countries are taking steps to improve budget procedures and introduce output or performance-oriented budgeting, although they are concerned about their capacity to implement such sophisticated systems. In 1998, the Fiji Government will introduce performance contracts for chief executives of departments. A state-of-the-art public

---

[6] A sharp and useful analytical perspective has been provided by Klitgaard (1996) who uses the equation C (corruption) = M (monopoly) + D (discretion) - A (accountability). The monopoly component can refer to any situation where the government or an official has the power to make a decision and those who are directly affected do not have an effective (competitive) alternative.

Box 2.1: Building Capability — Addressing Governance Issues

Development experience has shown that there is no uniquely superior form of governance. However, some common principles have emerged:

- Legislative, executive and judicial arms of government should be independent of one another.
- There should be a strong, independent judiciary.
- The administrative arm of government should be capable of providing independent technical advice.
- There should be a system of rules, processes and mechanisms that restrain corrupt behavior, ensure transparency and provide feedback to the government as a whole.

Normally, to be effective, the separation of powers needs to be formally incorporated. Formal separation of powers enhances confidence that the rules that constrain coercive power will remain stable. However, even if powers are formally separated, political leaders may not face effective checks and balances on their actions. The formal separation of powers must be complemented by other rules and mechanisms to ensure effective governance.

One of the most important components of an effective system of governance is a strong, independent judiciary. The judiciary must rule on the legality of the actions of the legislative and the executive arms of government. This is not possible where the legislature has the power to override or circumvent the decisions of the judiciary, for example, by arbitrarily changing judges or relying on customary arrangements that can dominate at an informal level. The judiciary also helps resolve contractual disputes, clarify legal ambiguities and enforce compliance of the general public. Hence, it must have the resources and the support of other branches of government to ensure compliance. However, general development experience suggests that independence and fairness are the most important characteristics of a strong judiciary.

There are various mechanisms that can be used to improve public sector and public enterprise performance that involve a careful balance between accountability and flexibility. Performance agreements, budgets transparency, clear and consistent objectives, independent monitoring and reporting, and other means of transmitting the objectives and performance of the public sector to the community are all important. External mechanisms can strengthen governance. There could be extraterritorial adjudication to underpin the domestic judicial system, or agreements with donors involving policy conditionality to provide accountability.

---

enterprise reform framework is already in place and there are plans to review the competition policy framework for both the public and private sectors.

In customs departments, generally there is potential for bribery if officials have discretion over valuation, if duty rates are high, and if there are wide variations for similar goods and specific exemptions. However, most Pacific Island countries are moving to a harmonized system and strengthening customs departments, which will reduce the scope for corruption problems and errors. Improved procedures include using data base systems that contain information on unit values, requirements to check export documentation from exporting countries, and greater ability to supervise computer entries. Nevertheless, fines and penalties for bribery are still too low to remove the incentives for bribery. Politicians have discretionary powers to grant exemptions from taxes and duties and to approve licenses, but there is no trans-

parent public reporting system to make them accountable for their decisions. This is a problem especially in foreign investment approval. Some governments have agreed to make investment guidelines more transparent, but discretionary, monopoly-type power often still exists and foreign investors have no effective means of ensuring accountability. Such situations leave room for corruption. If there is no transparent public reporting system, discretionary power should be removed.

Governance weaknesses that affect financial institutions and public enterprises can be particularly serious because of the burden they place on the budget if they fail. For example, the failure of the National Bank of Fiji and Polynesian Airlines in Samoa have placed significant demands on those country's budgets. Provisions that restrict pension funds to local investments provide too much temptation for corruption, particularly property investments. These and other examples have suggested the need to improve regulatory and performance monitoring for government and business enterprises. More generally, the Auditor General, Ombudsman Offices, the Judiciary and other entities with monitoring responsibilities must be independent or have independent reporting requirements and adequate fiscally protected resources.

In sum, improving governance would require:

- greater openness and public scrutiny of budgetary processes, public accounts, loan agreements, guarantees, public sector contracts and audits;

- progressive reduction and a movement toward uniformity of tariffs, and removal of exemptions of special treatment of specific industries, so as to minimize discretionary power;

- greater transparency in foreign investment approval processes; and

- strengthening of the judiciary and other regulatory bodies of government (e.g. Ombudsman, Auditor General) to deal with instances of corruption.

3. ENHANCING THE EFFECTIVENESS OF PUBLIC EXPENDITURES: SPENDING PATTERNS AND POLICIES

Enlarging the scope of the public sector produced some improvements in health, education and other social sectors in the Pacific Island Member Countries. But inefficient and overextended governments came under pressure beginning in the mid-1980s. Governments had become large and ungainly and were blamed for the disappointing average growth performance and people's continuing poor quality of life in some of the PMCs. Low growth hampered the governments' abilities to raise revenues. Fiscal deficits needed to be contained and macroeconomic stability maintained. Government could not improve services, and in some cases, could not even maintain them at the previous level. Expenditures were cut to restrain the deficit, but in an *ad hoc* manner, aggravated existing spending inefficiencies.

Kiribati has the highest ratio of government expenditure to GDP and its public enterprises dominate all economic activity. It was the first country to officially recognize that extensive public sector ownership and management was constraining development. In 1987, Kiribati announced an official policy of divestment. Since then, most of the PMCs, except for the Federated States of Micronesia and the Marshall Islands, have announced policies of comprehensive public sector reform. They intend to streamline the civil service, divest public enterprises and concentrate on core areas. The goal is to improve development effectiveness by making

government more cost-effective and clearing the way for the private sector to be the engine of economic growth. But despite good intentions, implementation of reforms has been delayed or watered down in most of the PMCs.

If private sector-led growth is to succeed, reforms must lead to public expenditure patterns consistent with macroeconomic stability and an environment conducive to efficient private economic activity. As discussed in Chapter 2, the state can improve the development effectiveness of public expenditure by limiting the scope of its activities to its capacity. However, concentrating public resources in core functions by itself does not guarantee development effectiveness. Spending policies also must be carefully balanced and coordinated.

BALANCING THE ECONOMIC COMPOSITION OF EXPENDITURE

In all of the PMCs there are two imbalances in the economic composition of expenditure: the first is between recurrent and investment expenditure, and the second is between the wage and nonwage components of recurrent expenditure. Both of these imbalances impede growth and development. For example, when there is a shortfall in the government's resources for current expenditure, fiscal adjustment often cuts development expenditure creating an imbalance between them. When the civil service wage bill is very large, existing government services and new asset accumulation are jeopardized because operations and maintenance allocations are inadequate.

In 1995, current expenditure exceeded 67 percent of total expenditure in all PMCs except Tonga and Vanuatu. In the Federated States of Micronesia (FSM) it was over 83 percent, and in Fiji, current expenditure soared to 88 percent of total expenditure. Most of it went directly to the governments' own wage bill, and indirectly—in the form of grants, subsidies and transfers—it often supported the wage bill in other government entities such as public enterprises. This curtailed operations and maintenance expenditure.

The extent of the shortfall and the imbalance between operations and maintenance and other current expenditure is difficult to assess in the aggregate. Each sector, subsector, or activity within each country has a different stock of capital and different operations and maintenance requirements. Recorded budgetary subsidies and equity transfers do not capture the full amount of government resources used to support inefficient public sector activities. The statutory authorities and public enterprises often receive significant indirect subsidies, such as tax exemptions or donor-funded grants and these are unlikely to be reflected in the budget.

Table 3. 1: Economic Composition of Government Expenditure in PMCs, 1995
(In percent of GDP)

	Wages	Interest	Other Current	Total Current	Development Exp. including Net Lending	Total Expenditure
Fiji	11.4	3.1	9.0	23.5	3.1	26.6
Kiribati	26.0	0.2	42.5	68.7	24.3	93.0
FSM	29.4	2.3	33.0	64.7	13.6	78.3
Marshall Islands	21.5	5.9	31.3	58.7	28.5	87.2
Samoa	11.7	1.3	17.8	30.8	38.3	69.1
Solomon Islands	10.9	4.1	14.2	29.2	14.4	43.6
Tonga	12.2	...	...	23.1	23.5	46.6
Vanuatu	11.9	0.7	13.7	26.3	12.8	39.1

Source: World Bank Regional Economic Reviews, Public Expenditure Reviews, and Country Economic Memoranda; IMF staff reports and Recent Economic Development Reports.

In Kiribati, according to government figures, budgetary subsidies to public enterprises are 3 percent of GDP, excluding tax exemptions. But *total* government support of public enterprises in 1996 is estimated to be closer to 7 percent of GDP.

A government grant to Air Kiribati in 1997 has pushed this figure to 10 percent of GDP. In Fiji, the government injected an average of F$25 million per year into public enterprises between 1992 and 1996 in the form of grants, loans and capital. The Government of Fiji has had a meager return on some investments and its share of public enterprise losses has averaged $13 million per year between 1994 and 1996. These resources—around 1.5 percent of GDP—have alternative uses that could yield much higher returns.

Underprovisioning for operations and maintenance is a chronic problem. Governments opt for a popular means of cutting expenditure, such as postponing operations and maintenance over an unpopular one, such as reducing the wage bill or raising user charges. Donors provide an inadvertent endorsement of this short-sighted approach by extending grant funds to replace or rehabilitate whatever has fallen apart for want of maintenance. Donors must accept considerable responsibility for this because they consistently reinforce the government's tendency to procrastinate on difficult political decisions required to balance current and development expenditure. As long as donors persist in this behavior, it makes no sense for the government to save money by cutting jobs or raising user fees. But these actions would be beneficial in the longer term.

This explains, in part, the low contribution of investment to growth in the PMCs. Another part of the puzzle may be that, in several countries, a large share of the development budget consists of equity injections into faltering public enterprises.

The effect of budget tightening on government investment is most pronounced in Fiji. In the early 1980s, central government development expenditure was 8 to 9 percent of GDP, but by 1990 fiscal adjustment had reduced this to 4 to 4.5 percent, and by 1995, development expenditure had dropped to 3 percent annually, a level which is generally considered too low to sustain the government's strategy of private sector-led growth.

Meanwhile, Fiji's current expenditure remains relatively unchanged at about 23 percent of GDP. Among the other PMCs, due to external grant funding, the development budget is more sensitive to the availability of donor funds than it is to the exigencies of fiscal adjustment. Fiji's 1996-97 development budget exemplifies the reason that returns on development expenditure remain low in the PMCs. The Government of Fiji provided funds to bail out depositors of NBF and to increase the budget for agriculture; neither of these budgetary allocations is likely to result in high growth.

Evidence shows that high levels of current expenditure are a drag on growth, especially when excessive share of current expenditure goes to the wage bill or for subsidies.[1] The drag effect on growth is also more pronounced when the public sector constitutes a large part of the economy, and the wage bill is large relative to GDP. The larger the wage bill relative to the economy, the larger the proportion of economic resources which may be inefficiently employed. In the PMCs, the average government wage bill for 1990-95 ranged

---

[1] Of course, some types of current expenditure, such as teachers' salaries, may actually raise development effectiveness.

from 10 percent of GDP in Tonga to 30 percent in FSM. This type of expenditure typically crowds out operations and maintenance; services deteriorate for lack of supplies; public assets deteriorate for lack of maintenance; and the return to investments is far lower than expected.

PUBLIC EXPENDITURE REFORM: EASIER SAID THAN DONE

To improve the development effectiveness of expenditure, PMC governments must *carry out* the reforms they have announced—streamlining government, public enterprise and the civil service. Fiji is in the process of reform, but opposition from the civil service unions delays the reforms somewhat. The Solomon Islands, Samoa and Vanuatu have announced their intention to undertake reforms.

Improving the quality of development expenditure will require better planning, project preparation, assessment and selection, in the initial context of a medium-term Public Sector Investment Program (PSIP) (see Chapter 4). The annual development budgets drawn from the PSIP should be derived from government policies and priorities; should be designed to complement and support government's current and planned service levels, and should be well integrated with the recurrent budget.

If government reduces the size of the civil service, the balance between the wage bill, other current expenditure and development expenditure will improve. The civil service and its remuneration must become more flexible in hiring practices and a performance-oriented reward system should be adopted.

IMPROVING INTRASECTORAL EXPENDITURE: HEALTH, EDUCATION AND INFRASTRUCTURE

HEALTH. Virtually all health care in the PMCs is provided and financed by government with substantial donor assistance. Although health indicators have improved in the PMCs over the past 20 years, the health care system suffers from several problems. On average, PMC government spending on health in the 1990s has been well above health spending for countries at similar income levels. Most of the PMC governments' health expenditures experienced substantial changes over the period.[2] By 1996, health expenditure was between 10 and 17 percent of current expenditure (table 3.2).

There is a sustained bias toward curative care, hospital-provided preventive care and primary care. This makes the health care system less cost effective. For example, in Kiribati, most diseases are preventable and the official policy is to emphasize primary and preventive care. Nevertheless, in the recurrent budget for 1997, curative services take up 76.5 percent of the total recurrent budget. In Tonga, the hospital share of the health budget is 60 percent. In Fiji, about 50 percent of the Ministry of Health's budget is for urban hospitals, about 15 percent for drugs and supplies, and only 2 percent for public health services.

User charges for health services are inadequate—and aggravate the lack of cost effectiveness. In Kiribati, there is a small charge for beds in a private ward in the main hospital. In Vanuatu, user charges have been eliminated. In Samoa there is a low fee schedule for curative services. Cost

---

2 Information on total government health spending was not available for this report for most PMC countries. The analysis therefore relies on statistics on governments' current expenditure for health.

recovery in the PMCs' health systems is estimated at between 0.5 and 4 percent.[3]

Table 3.2: Government Current Expenditure on Health, 1990-96

Country	Percent of Current Govt. Expenditure		Percent of GDP	
	Av. 1990-95	1996	Av. 1990-95	1996
Fiji [1]	9.9	12.5	2.8	3.8
Kiribati	16.1	17.0	9.0	10.7
FSM [2]	14.0	14.0	...	...
Marshall Islands [3]	10.8	10.6	6.6	6.2
Samoa [4]	14.3	15.8	2.7	4.1
Solomon Islands [2]	11.0	10.2	...	2.9
Tonga [1]	12.4	13.3	3.9	4.2
Vanuatu [3]	10.5	10.4	2.3	2.2

Source: World Bank Public Expenditure Review Country Economic Memoranda and Regional Economic Reports; IMF Recent Economic Development Reports and data provided by the authorities.
1/ Total health expenditure in percent of total government expenditure.
2/ Estimated, based on World Bank CEM 1993. Solomon Islands for 1996 is actual.
3/ Statistics in 1996 column is actual for 1995.
4/ Net of VAT.

Government resources are concentrated on expensive curative and hospital services in cities, and prevention; access to health care in rural areas is poor or non-existent. This is at odds with the Government's policy to alleviate poverty. In Tonga, for example, only about 13 percent of the health budget is directed toward rural areas. In the Solomon Islands, the Ministry of Health provides only a small portion of the budget for preventive and promotive programs.[4] Preventive programs for the most common disease in Solomon Islands—malaria—is largely dependent on donor funding.

Most of the health budget goes to salaries, resulting in shortages of medical supplies and, thus, resulting in no provision for maintenance. For example, in Vanuatu, salaries absorb 68 percent, while

---

[3] See World Bank: Pacific Island Economies: Towards Efficient and Sustainable Growth, Vol. 1 (1993).

[4] Solomon Islands, Ministry of Health and Medical Services: The Comprehensive Review of Health Services Report (March 1996).

pharmaceuticals and supplies make up only 12 percent of the budget; in Samoa, the figures are 54 and 19 percent. In the hospitals, health care suffers from poorly maintained equipment. There is little integration between the current and the development budget. As a result, many preventive programs, which governments have declared top-priorities, are funded by donors through the development budget. This is the case in the Solomon Islands' bednet program for malaria prevention. Meanwhile, national governments continue to concentrate their scarce resources on much higher cost curative services.

Despite heavy government expenditures, basic health care needs in all the PMC are largely unmet. But in this area, the social returns are the highest, and government involvement is crucial in public and preventive care, especially in rural parts of the country.

Government should not provide or finance all health care. The challenge for governments is to concentrate resources in a cost-effective way: on public goods (see Chapter 2) and basic services that will benefit the poor and that have the highest social returns including high externalities. To do this, governments should establish goals, a strategy to reach them, and plan to implement the strategy based on the best input combinations. Governments should scale back their direct responsibilities in other aspects of health care.

Public health and preventive care require a different focus in each country according to their health status. For example, in Kiribati, public health education in sanitation is most necessary; in Tonga lifestyle-related diseases are at the forefront; whereas in Solomon Islands, public health education could help bring malaria under control at low cost by educating the population about the benefit of properly maintained bednets.[5] Greater participation by local community groups offers a cost-effective means of public health dissemination. In Samoa, for example, 60 percent of those surveyed in a pilot study stated that they acquired health knowledge through their peers and acquaintances (see Annex 4). Thus, the challenge is to meaningfully include local leaders in public health campaigns.

The budget allocation between wages, supplies, maintenance and investment should be guided by cost/benefit considerations which will achieve the objective at the lowest cost.

For example, government might reduce its direct involvement by regulating or permitting private management or even ownership of health care facilities by physicians, NGOs and church groups, even in core government activities. In the 1997 budget, Fiji reduced health sector costs by contracting out cleaning services, transportation, catering, and laundry, among other services.

Other savings can be realized by increasing cost recovery, especially in tertiary curative services which are relatively high cost and offer fewer benefits to society. Fiji has plans to increase cost recovery, but the initial cost recovery rate will be only an estimated 2.5 percent of the health budget.

The PMC Governments should also encourage increased use of health insurance, initially limited to coverage of major illnesses. So far, the Marshall Islands has a Social Security Health Insurance, and Fiji has a fledgling private health insurance, but establishing user charges for medical services will provide incentives for health insurance in other PMCs.

---

5   See World Bank, Kiribati: Public Expenditure Review 1997; Tonga, Public Expenditure Review 1997; Comprehensive Health Sector Review.

Governments and donors should work together to ensure that health projects funded through the development budget not only support government priorities, but are integrated with and complement current expenditure. Project evaluation should be strengthened to ensure that investment projects are based on established priorities, screened, and undergo thorough project preparation process, followed up by stronger monitoring and control by the PMC governments.

EDUCATION. The institutional arrangements and financing for education vary among the PMCs and there are many combinations of public and private participation and funding. In general, the government is either the sole or principal provider of primary education; secondary education is often dominated by private schools, many of which are run by religious organizations. In-country vocational and tertiary education is also provided and mainly funded by the PMC governments. External education is funded by scholarships, frequently with donor assistance. For example, in Fiji, most primary and secondary schools are private, and teachers are paid primarily by government. In FSM, secondary schools are government-owned.

Like health care expenditure, PMCs' government expenditure on education varies among the countries; there have been significant changes over the 1990s. Kiribati's education expenditure, already high relative to GDP, has been increasing steadily, with a relatively constant share of the current expenditure. In Fiji, Solomon Islands and the Marshall Islands, the fiscal adjustment in the 1990s resulted in a decline in education expenditure relative to GDP. In Fiji, in 1995 salaries accounted for 78 percent of expenditure in the sector, maintenance and operations for 0.5 percent and textbooks, supplies and materials for 2.9 percent. In Tonga, the latter provision was 1.5 percent.

Table 3.3 summarizes PMC government expenditure on education, relative to GDP and to current expenditure. By international standards, most of the PMCs have higher levels of expenditure on education relative to GDP. Furthermore, education in the PMC countries tends to be expensive because of the high cost of internal transport arising from the fragmentation of the land mass of each island nation. The question whether the present basic education system (primary and junior secondary schools) is developing the skills appropriate to the formal and subsistence economies of the island-states has not yet been conclusively addressed.

Educational outcomes in all the PMCs except Tonga are poor in developing required skills, but especially so since education accounts for more than a quarter of public expenditure when government, donor and private financing are taken into account. In many of the PMCs, access to education is limited. Primary education is not compulsory, except for Tonga, Fiji and the Marshall Islands. Recently, in most

Increasing access has exacerbated the inferior quality of education. Student drop-out and repeat rates have increased and elevated the already high cost of education. By the time students graduate from primary school, they are several years behind same-age students in industrial countries. In Fiji, FSM, Marshall Islands and Samoa, only about half of the students who finish primary school go on to secondary education and in the rest of the PMCs, the numbers are much lower, ranging from 17 percent in Vanuatu to 7 percent in Kiribati.

The key to improved development effectiveness of education expenditure is to focus government resources on activities with the highest social returns and externalities. Providing quality universal primary education using the most cost effective input combination—possibly a mix of private and public education comes first. Primary education has high social returns. Children find it difficult to catch up with educational achievement later. Unless there is good primary education, further schooling

Table 3.3: Government Expenditure on Education, 1990-96

	In percent of current govt. expenditure		In percent of GDP	
	Av. 1990-95	1996	Av. 1990-95	1996
Fiji 1/	19.4	14.3	5.5	4.4
Kiribati	20.4	20.9	11.2	13.2
FSM	...	...	...	...
Marshall Islands 2/	14.8	16.6	11.0	9.7
Samoa	18.2	17.5	5.2	4.5
Solomon Islands 3/	17.0	14.6	5.3	4.2
Tonga	18.7	18.3	9.8	9.8
Vanuatu 2/	22.2	23.2	4.9	5.0

Source: World Bank Regional Economic Reviews, Public Expenditure Reviews, and Country Economic Memoranda; IMF staff reports and Recent Economic Development Reports.
1/ Total education expenditure in percent of total government expenditure.;
2/ For Marshall Islands and Vanuatu, shares in 1996 column are 1995 actuals;
3/ Average for 1990-93.

PMCs, access to primary education has increased rapidly, but there are insufficient qualified teachers, textbooks, and schools.

is likely to yield low returns, as experience in the PMCs confirms. Also, returns to education are especially high at the primary level because universal basic literacy yields large externalities. Educating girls, for example, is linked to better health for women and their children, and lower fertility rates.[6]

At the same time, the governments should ensure that post-primary students, who now swell enrollments in primary schools in Fiji, Vanuatu and the Solomon Islands, have access to continuing education. Recently, the pressure of these post-primary students has led to the sharp increase in community day schools in the Solomon Islands. Since financial, material, and human resources vary among the PMCs, the optimum strategy for primary and post primary education will differ for each country. Where government resources are very limited, post-primary students might be accommodated by expanding secondary education through partnerships with church groups and the private sector which are already heavily involved in secondary education in most PMCs. If the government subsidized existing or new private secondary schools it would be more cost-effective than establishing government-funded secondary schools as cost recovery of private schools is high. In Kiribati, the planned expansion of government involvement in secondary education has left uncertain the future role of the churches in the sector which seems inconsistent with improving cost-effectiveness of education expenditure.

Students who pursue tertiary education are likely to earn higher incomes later. But cost recovery mechanisms are virtually nonexistent in the PMCs and should be developed as is being done in Fiji. Instead of funding post-secondary training abroad, government and donor assistance should be channeled to the government's core activities in basic education. Government

and donors should also refrain from establishing or funding educational institutions outside these activities since such funding will preempt resources to core activities. In particular, the establishment of national universities should be avoided in the PMCs, as they would divert and absorb resources which should be allocated to basic education.

These recommendations would dramatically reconfigure intrasectoral distribution of education expenditure directing most funding for primary education. For example, in Fiji and Tonga, only 40 percent of current expenditure in education goes to primary education and about 30 percent goes to secondary education in Fiji, and 22 percent to secondary education in Tonga. In Tonga's 1994/95 budget, one third of the total education budget was for development expenditure owing to donor-funded scholarships for training abroad.

PHYSICAL INFRASTRUCTURE. In the PMCs, roads, sea defenses, air and seaports, and utilities, have been provided and paid for by the public sector, with extensive donor support. Infrastructure services are almost entirely publicly financed. The institutional arrangements vary among the PMCs, but generally, the government includes investment in the sector as part of the development budget. Service is provided partly by government ministries or departments, and partly by non-financial public enterprises, such as the Fiji Electricity Authority (FEA) in Fiji and the Public Utilities Board (PUB) in Kiribati. In addition to investments in the sector, government expenditure includes the operating and maintenance costs for services such as current operations, subsidies and equity injections which may be included on the government's capital account as part of its net lending.

Public investment in infrastructure has been heavy, including equity injections to State-

---

6 World Development Report 1997.

owned enterprises. In Tonga, an average of 43 percent of overall development expenditure has supported infrastructure since 1980. In Samoa, the infrastructure share of development expenditure has been even higher at about 45 percent—equivalent to an average of about 15 percent of GDP since 1991. In part this is due to the damage caused by cyclones in 1990 and 1991. In Fiji, between 1990 and 1995, the average share of infrastructure in government capital expenditure was 44 percent.

Despite the importance and scale of public investment in the sector, access to basic public services remains limited in most of the PMCs and service provision is poor. In Tonga, telecommunications are seriously inadequate, water supply is a major development constraint, and power outages are frequent. In Kiribati, the Public Utility Board (PUB) covers essentially only part of Tarawa, and even in this limited area there are frequent power problems, breakdowns and outages; water delivery is sporadic and water quality is questionable; and the sewerage system is in constant need of repair. Telecommunications services exist only in Tarawa.

These problems exist and persist because existing assets suffer from lack of maintenance and inadequate allocations for operations. This leads to low yield on prior investments and insufficient funds for new investment to expand services. Many interrelated factors contribute to the situation. Departments and agencies are overstaffed, cost recovery policies are inadequate, and there are no funds for maintenance. In Kiribati, the Public Utility Board's tariffs have not changed since 1990, except that the water charge was rescinded in 1996, when the service collapsed. Sewerage disposal is provided free of charge. In Solomon Islands, the few paved roads, including the main road through Honiara, are disintegrating because they are not being maintained. In Samoa and in Kiribati, there is a *de facto* government policy of deferred maintenance such that maintenance allocations are a fraction of required amounts because, based on experience, governments expect that donors will eventually rehabilitate or replace assets.

In the PMCs, there are many examples of public entities which impede growth and development, rather than support it. Infrastructure is no exception. The management is inefficient, the staff is too large, and public pricing policy does not reflect costs. Limited resources and lack of incentives constrain the entities' ability to undertake needed maintenance or expand capacity to improve both access and quality of services. As a result, the entities become a drain on the government budget.

In the early 1990s, the Fiji Electricity Authority (FEA) was an example of such an entity. FEA operations have since been commercialized and the energy sector in Fiji is about to be deregulated which will permit independent power providers. This should encourage competition and reduce cost. Fiji is also planning to commercialize the Government's Water and Sewerage Department soon. The government is tendering some road maintenance and construction to the private sector to increase its cost-effectiveness.

The PMCs must provide more and better service to support private sector development. Governments have generally recognized the need to improve efficiency, but they have been slow to implement changes because of political considerations and difficulties in reducing the work-force and raising user charges. Providing adequate maintenance and recovering this cost is also complicated by donors' preference for funding rehabilitation and construction works. Because most of these funds are grants, expensive rehabilitation work is made available at no cost. As long as donors are willing to hand out funds, no rational government would choose to spend its own resources on maintenance.

International experience suggests that the PMCs can improve the contribution of infrastructure to growth by managing the sector on commercial principles in an environment of direct or indirect competition. Government can greatly improve the development effectiveness of its expenditure in the area by concentrating its resources in those areas with the highest social returns and large externalities and providing the environment for private sector participation in the infrastructure sector on commercial principles. Direct private or public sector involvement can be managed on commercial terms with cost recovery (including agreed support from government where such support is necessary to establish commercial operations) set at a level sufficient to cover their cost, including an adequate return on assets.

When the PMCs divest components of the infrastructure sector, they must create regulations to ensure that a public monopoly is not replaced by a private one. This would merely restrict output and increase price and profits. Although recent advances in technology have reduced the natural monopolies in power generation and telecommunications, the PMCs' size makes monopolistic behavior more easily attainable.

CONCLUSIONS

PMC governments can improve the development effectiveness of expenditure by narrowing the range of their responsibilities in key areas and providing the services in the most cost-effective way. As a result, public sector reform should focus government expenditure on public goods or services in health, education, and infrastructure which reduce or alleviate poverty, and deliver high externalities and high rates of social return. Reforms should also aim to improve the cost effectiveness of government services by providing the most cost-effective input combination, including high quality investments and efficient operation and maintenance. To accomplish this, governments must adopt a medium-term budgetary frame-work and grant more freedom to spending agencies; they must also ensure that managers have sufficient budgeting and resource management skills to be held accountable for their decisions.

4. PLANNING AND BUDGETING FOR MORE EFFECTIVE SPENDING

SIGNPOSTS ON THE PATH TO REFORM

Well-functioning planning and budgetary systems are central to the performance of government and the achievement of economic reform goals. Like most developing countries, the PMCs have relied upon a traditional, centralized budget system. But the emergence of fiscal deficits, and the realization that some traditional sources of funding may be disappearing, have led the PMC governments to examine how their budget systems can better support their development goals.

As a result, some of the PMCs are now considering budgetary reform while others are at different stages of implementing variants of output or performance budgeting, which, for the purpose of this chapter, are grouped under the term "performance-oriented budgeting."[1] A few of the PMCs

have yet to begin. Fiji is the most advanced in implementing performance-oriented budgeting, and has a clear agenda for further change. Others, such as Kiribati, Tonga, and Samoa still have major hurdles to overcome on their paths to reform. The Solomon Islands and Vanuatu have recognized a need to change to a budget system which emphasizes accountability for results. The Solomon Islands is operating under a traditional budget system, but the accounting, information and control systems have broken down, rendering the budget ineffective.

This chapter discusses some of the issues involved in budget reform, and provides some pointers for the next steps of budget reform in the PMCs.

THE TRADITIONAL BUDGET SYSTEM: THE STANDARD AGAINST WHICH REFORMS SHOULD BE MEASURED

The traditional budget system found in the Solomon Islands and many other PMCs has

---

[1] A performance budget is usually associated with a budget classification that divides proposed expenditures into activities within each organization, and into a set of workload measures that relate the activity performed to its cost.

Performance budgeting allows the budget to be built, not incrementally (as in traditional line-item budgeting), but on the basis of anticipated workload. Managers could arrive at a budget by simply multiplying the cost of a unit of output by the number of units needed in the next year. The bottom-up approach of performance budgeting, however, is expansionary unless it is constrained by strong top-down control of aggregate ceilings, and tradeoffs are made between program output levels. Performance budgeting was developed in the United States in the 1950s, and continues to be used by a number of city governments in that country. Elements of performance budgeting can be found in some developing country

budgets in the form of performance information output levels or targets.

Output budgeting is most often associated with the New Zealand public management reforms of the 1980s and 1990s, which are built around contractual relationships between ministries as purchasers of goods and services, and departments as providers. Appropriation in the budget are for outputs, and in providing those outputs, departments have considerable flexibility in the use of inputs, subject to rigorous financial and output reporting.

two distinctive features. The first is that the budget is assembled and implemented on a line-item basis. The second is its dual structure. In line-item budgeting, core ministries dominate budget preparation, and during the budget year, spending ministries have only limited authority to move funds between items within the same heads and sub-heads. The traditional budget system focuses on the cost of inputs—expenditures on wages, travel, purchases, maintenance, investments and so forth—and whether budgetary expenditures match budgetary allocations. In most cases, the results—or outputs—of budgetary expenditures are not evaluated as part of the formal budget process. The advantages of line-item budgeting are that the strong central control and limited line agency discretion minimizes the potential for line agency overspending, avoids capricious and inconsistent decision-making, and reduces the risks of corruption. It is also straightforward and robust, and facilitates the control of spending.

However, there are many disadvantages. Strong central control weakens incentives for line agencies to reduce spending on line items already in the budget in order to fund new priorities with the savings; it encourages line agencies to *dispense* funds rather than plan for their optimal use and it reduces line agency capacity to implement internal reallocations. Budgeting also typically becomes incremental —last year's allocation is the floor on which this year's budget is constructed. As a result, a bias develops in the budget toward the *status quo* in that it is easier to preserve existing activities than it is to fund new ones. Likewise, it is easier to postpone outlays not yet in the budget than it is to reduce the scale of current activities; it is easier to withhold budgetary discretion from agency line managers than it is to develop their capacity to exercise this freedom; and it is easier to monitor input costs and budgetary expenditures against allocations, than it is to monitor the efficiency and effectiveness of

budgetary funds in achieving government priorities.2 Against this background, it is understandable that the PMCs have been exploring ways in which budgeting systems can be better adapted to meeting the challenges posed by rekindling economic growth and re-orienting government.

A second characteristic of traditional budgeting in developing countries is a dual structure: the division of the budget into two parts. Dual budgets emerged around the time of independence as a practical way of managing the growing volume of aid financing and the political desire of governments to pursue a strategy of government-led development. The development effectiveness of public expenditure is hampered in the PMCs by the way the recurrent and the development budgets have evolved and are separately prepared.3 The recurrent expenditure requirements of investments are not rigorously estimated when projects are prepared, and thus the affordability of the programs of which they are a part over the longer term is not properly considered. This leads to inadequate provision for expenditures in subsequent budgets, and unsustainable investment decisions. The development budget often does not include investment activities required to sustain services specified by the government's policies and priorities. Institutional responsibilities are typically divided. For

---

2 Countries with traditional budget systems may still evaluate results either by separate monitoring and evaluation units, or by requiring department heads to publish an annual report on their department's activities.

3 In all PMCs which still maintain separate recurrent and development budgets, the recurrent budget includes domestically funded expenditures of recurrent nature, while the development budget includes all externally funded expenditures, regardless of their nature, and a small amount of domestic funding of development expenditure. Thus, although the development budget appears at first glance to be an investment budget, in reality it is an aid budget.

example, in the Solomon Islands, the Ministry of Finance prepares and monitors the recurrent budget, and the Ministry of National Planning and Development prepares and monitors the development budget. Each budget is submitted separately to Parliament and little effort is made to integrate the two.

Furthermore, there are problems with prioritization, planning, and technical preparation of development expenditures that have hampered effectiveness. For example, projects are not integrated with the government's policies and priorities *or* the current budget; and virtually no central or line agency has the capacity for project preparation. Instead, the government relies on donors for technical assistance to prepare and appraise projects, and to fund most of the development budget. As a result, the development budget is largely driven by donors because government priorities are not well-established. One way to regain control over such projects is to prepare a Public Sector Investment Program (PSIP), but this requires the government to adhere to the discipline of a PSIP in making annual budgets and in negotiating external aid. In the Solomon Islands, for example, there have been several unsuccessful efforts to improve the development budget by establishing a three year PSIP from which well-prepared and prioritized projects can be drawn.

CHARACTERISTICS OF WELL-PERFORMING BUDGETS

A useful way of looking at a country's budget system is to assess its effectiveness at three levels. The first level is the capacity of the budget to articulate and fulfill the government's aggregate fiscal objectives. Ministries of finance, working with the central bank, typically establish a fiscal framework within which budgets can be framed and monitored. The capacity of the

budget to achieve the targets, on the revenue and particularly on the expenditure side, and, of course, for the overall fiscal balance is critical to macroeconomic stability. Line-item budgets, with their emphasis on central control, often do well at controlling spending within fiscal targets. Decentralized budget systems, which give managers more flexibility in the use of resources, carry high risks unless they are accompanied by strong financial reporting based on sound accounting systems.

The second level of effective budgeting is the budget's capacity to allocate resources based on strategic priorities. This means prioritizing competing claims on scarce resources. Prioritization is fundamentally a political process. The challenge is to structure institutional arrangements to both inform and force tradeoffs between alternative policy programs and projects, within a hard budget constraint. Line-item budgets, being incremental, are generally poor at reflecting strategic priorities, although if they are linked to a strong national planning process, this can be counteracted. Budgets that focus on results have the potential of being more effective. However, dual budget systems that have separate development budgets derived from a PSIP and are driven by high aid flows can be fiscally dynamic over time, leading to budgetary failure at the first level.

The third level is operational efficiency and effectiveness, i.e. whether the budget supports the delivery of programs and projects. This requires both human and financial resources commensurate with the tasks to be performed. It requires clarity in those tasks, authority to pursue the purpose and undertake the task, and accountability for the use of that authority. Traditional line-item budget systems can achieve operational efficiency and effectiveness if the country has a well-motivated public service, and the budget is buttressed by departmental reporting and evaluation systems. Without these accompaniments, traditional line-item budgeting provides weak incentives for operational efficiency and effectiveness—although it may encourage economy. Performance-oriented budget systems have a greater potential for operational efficiency, but need to be part of a broader set of incentives for good performance. Budget change alone will not achieve improved performance, a reality overlooked by many of the earlier attempts by developing countries to build budgets on the basis of workloads.

PERFORMANCE-ORIENTED BUDGETING: POTENTIAL FOR IMPROVEMENT BUT NOT A PANACEA

Countries which have sought to move beyond traditional line-item budgeting with the objective of improving performance have taken steps such as: (1) recasting the budget into a program structure; (2) developing performance measures and incorporating them into the budget document; (3) preparing a medium-term budgetary framework; (4) strengthening financial management systems, and in some cases, adopting partial or full accrual accounting; (5) creating 'broad-banded' categories for expenditures; and (6) devolving discretionary spending to line ministries. They have also sought to link planning and budgeting more closely, either by strengthening the PSIP and its role in the preparation of the development budget, or, in some cases, abolishing the dual budget structure and integrating both current and investment spending into a unitary budget document prepared under the direction of a single budgetary authority.

Several of these main features of budgetary reform are present—in varying degrees—among the PMCs. Reform emphasizes outputs and performance, as well as

knowing the full cost of programs, including investment and the use of capital in order to get "value for money." In this regard, Fiji has taken the lead to unify the development budget and the recurrent budget, and to introduce accrual accounting.

PROGRAM FORMATS AND PERFORMANCE MEASURES

Fully fledged program budgeting was one of the principal public management exports from industrialized to developing countries in the 1960s and 1970s. It involves reorganizing the budget around policies and the resources needed to implement them—a departure from traditional budgeting based on organizational structure. It was an attempt to budget by making choices among competing policies, informed by estimates of the economic costs and benefits of policies and programs. In turn, this implied outcome measurement systems. Program budgeting never really succeeded in industrial countries, and failed dismally in developing countries. This was partly due to the lack of information available to policymakers on program outcomes, but mostly because program budgeting requires a high degree of political commitment to its internal discipline. Budgets are primarily political documents, not exercises in economic cost/benefit analysis.

Since then, a growing number of governments have pursued a less ambitious form of program budgeting, in which departmental budgets are cast in program format to aid transparency and policy choice, but no attempt is made to make cost/benefit analysis of policies and programs the central tool of budget preparation.

Budgets in program format aid transparency. They also may facilitate the introduction of output targets and performance measurement indicators to the budget document, bridging the gap between program and performance budgeting. Therefore, governments may convert budgets to program format as one of the steps in moving toward a more performance-oriented system of budgeting. Some PMCs have done this.

likelihood that adjustments in the bottom line will be made by choice rather than being forced by external circumstances; it provides a longer time frame for the agencies to reprioritize resources and plan adjustments; it helps the government to better integrate the annual budget with its

---

Box 4.1: Strengthening Budgeting through a Medium-Term Expenditure Framework

Resource allocation is about choice and, as such, is fundamentally political. The challenge is to design institutional arrangements that encourage strategic policymaking based on affordability, foster more cost-effective performance, and create an environment where public service providers have greater predictability and can thus plan for the medium term.

The central coordinating role of the budget has been weakened in many countries because it has been delinked from policymaking and planning. The result has often been budgets that are unrealistic or have little relation to expressed strategic priorities. A Medium-Term Expenditure Framework is an institutional device that formally and transparently tries to link policy, planning and budgeting. If used well, it enhances the capacity of government to maintain aggregate fiscal discipline while prioritizing (and, if needed, reallocating) resources to reflect changing strategic priorities. An MTEF imposes the following "rules of the game":

- an aggregate budget constraint defines what overall envelope of resources is available;
- policy proposals must compete with one another—both as ideas and for funding over the medium term, and what is demanded must be reconciled with what is affordable;
- proposals for policies and projects must be accompanied by cost and results information over the medium term; and
- evaluation influences resource allocation decisions and provides information to drive improvements in the quality of service delivery.

Evidence from both OECD countries and a growing number of developing countries that have introduced MTEFs shows that institutional reforms along these lines can contribute to fiscal discipline, better allocation of resources, and improved service delivery.

MAKING BUDGETS IN A MEDIUM-TERM FRAMEWORK

Performance-oriented reforms often require that the annual budget is prepared within a medium-term framework. A Medium-Term Expenditure Framework (MTEF) helps improve performance, particularly at the first two levels, but also, indirectly, at the third level. An MTEF makes the medium-term consequences of running budget deficits more transparent; it increases the

medium-term development plan; and it enables individual spending proposals to be evaluated on the basis of their life cycle budget impact. By making the cost of policies transparent over time, and by enabling them to be compared with the available resources, an MTEF can be an essential planning tool to help countries rein in the functions of government and ensure that resources are concentrated on priority programs.

BROAD-BANDING AND DECENTRALIZATION OF SPENDING AUTHORITY

Budget reform may also entail changes which improve the performance of budgets in regard to their optimal efficiency and effectiveness. Performance-oriented budgets generally group closely related activities into programs that contribute to a common policy objective. The aim is to allow managers flexibility within the 'broad-band' of line items to manage their human and financial resources and achieve a specified outcome in the most cost-effective manner.

In fact, the benefits of performance-oriented budgeting may not be forthcoming if departments and agencies are restricted in the discretionary power they have over resources. Devolution of authority enables line agencies to select the most efficient and effective means of using existing resources; it also allows them to respond more rapidly to changes such as shortcomings in program delivery or shifts in the program environment.

However, a note of caution is in order. Devolving authority to lower levels to facilitate better use of resources *can work only if there is sufficient managerial capacity*. This has not been the case in many of the PMCs. Managerial and accounting systems shortcomings have led to problems in implementing budgetary reform in both Kiribati and Samoa. In Kiribati, the move to performance-oriented budgeting led initially to sharp expenditure increases, and other problems resulting from limited understanding of the system. It was difficult to define outputs, and both the central and the line ministries' staff lacked training, cost information, and financial management skills. In Samoa, line ministries had only limited information and understanding of the reform process which curtailed participation in the budgetary process. Greater delegation of spending authority to managers also

requires strong financial reporting systems and well-entrenched accounting capacity. In the experience of other countries which have successfully decentralized budgeting, reforms in financial management have been a critical prior step.

STRENGTHENING THE PSIP

The PSIP has become a standard planning tool for a dual budget system in many developing countries. However, over the years, some concerns have been raised about the effects of PSIPs on budgeting over time where there are large volumes of external aid, a characteristic of development budgets in the PMCs. A weakness of the traditional PSIP model is that it can give an expansionary bias to government expenditures. Insufficient attention is paid to the financial costs the government will have to bear once external support has ended. The costs of operating the project as a program must then be borne from local revenues through the recurrent budget.

There are four "golden rules" for the sustainable operation of a PSIP/DB model of budget planning and preparation which practitioners have sought to follow. The first is that there should be limits on the overall size of the PSIP. Assuming a fairly even spread of projects across government ministries, the PSIP should typically be no more than one-quarter to one-third of the recurrent budget, otherwise the recurrent expenditures arising from completed investment projects in future years may overwhelm the recurrent budget. The second is that projects entering the PSIP must generally pass an economic viability test, such as a threshold economic rate of return. The third is that the incremental budgetary recurrent costs should be estimated as accurately as possible, and related to the underlying budgetary capacity of the sponsoring department. The fourth rule, violated in many developing countries outside the Pacific Region, is that economic policies should be pursued that foster the growth of the government's revenue base. If these rules are violated and aid flows are large, a vicious circle ensues—government commitments and staffing expand, provision for operating costs decline, as do civil service salaries. There are signs of this happening in the PMCs. Ultimately, the development budget becomes an aid budget, donor "projects" become programs of investment rehabilitation and current support, and the true investment component of the budget falls. In this way, perversely, a PSIP/DB model, if not controlled in the face of high aid flows, over time may lead to levels of public investment *below* what is required for sustainable growth.

Efforts to strengthen the PSIP across the developing world have increasingly focused on re-asserting the basics of good PSIP management, as reflected in these rules. While it is clearly not possible to estimate the economic rate of return of all projects, the role of economic analysis is now defined more as a test of the viability of controversial large projects, and as a mechanism to facilitate choice between similar alternatives within a sector. There is greater recognition that projects should be selected against a range of criteria, both economic and non-economic, and in particular, the chosen role of the government in the sector. There is also greater emphasis on the recurrent budget as the starting point. The development budget should consist of the capital budget, so to speak, plus program-related spending in the recurrent budget, putting policy and programs first. And related to this is the recognition that the PSIP and both parts of the budget should be integrated in some sort of MTEF. In this way the PSIP is becoming less of an economic planner's interpretation of what should constitute public investment, and more of a tool to manage public expenditures, and in particular external financing.

However, PSIPs are absent in budgeting systems of the main OECD countries, which also have unitary rather than dual budgets. Eventually, the PMCs may want to consider unifying their present dual structures, thereby forcing departments' investment and current spending demands to compete with one another against a single hard budget constraint.

DIRECTIONS FOR BUDGETARY REFORM

Fiji and Samoa are the only countries among the PMCs which have adopted a medium-term budget framework, including budget estimates. Fiji and Kiribati have made progress in their budget estimates for 1997 including, for the first time, output targets and activity descriptions. However, neither has completed the transformation to performance budgeting. In Fiji, program and activity costing is still mostly in line-item form. In Kiribati, output specification and measurable indicators need further work, and the budget supplement presents the detailed inputs in the traditional way which means that managers continue to operate much the same as they did under the traditional budget system. Performance-oriented budgets have been adopted in principle by Fiji, Samoa and Kiribati while Tonga has just begun the process. Fiji now presents a unified budget consisting of programs and activities and is introducing accrual accounting. However, Fiji's budget remains heavily input-oriented. Formally, Samoa also uses a unified budget, and is considering the introduction of accrual accounting. In Kiribati, the output budget format has been introduced, but without the full integration of the development budget, and the accounting system is still on a cash basis.

Figure 4.1: State of Reforms in Selected PMCs

	Current Budget Reform Status	Suggested Steps to Progress on Budget Reform
Fiji	In Place: Unified budget: programs and activities include both recurrent and capital expenditure. Input-oriented budget, with some output orientation from 1997. Increased focus on output targets from 1998. Medium- term, 3-year framework for the budget for each activity and program. Broad banding of line items in the budget. Corporate Planning. Accrual accounting piloted in 4 ministries. Training of senior public sector executives in management skills and close work with spending agencies in need of capability building. Scheduled for 1998: Performance agreement and 5-year contracts with each Permanent Secretary. Greater freedom for Permanent Secretaries to decide on resources in their agencies, including delegation of power by Public Service Commission to allow agency heads to appoint staff up to middle management level.	Focus on sharpening output targets. Train managers in financial and policy skills. Implement full accrual accounting in the long term. Initiate performance contracts for middle management.
Kiribati	In Place: Output budget introduced formally. Training in output budget preparation and development of key performance indicators. Improvements in the Financial Management System. Scheduled for 1998: Linking of the capital and recurrent expenditure in the output budget format.	Improve cost and accounting systems. Train staff in both the central and the line agencies to improve financial and policy management skills. Focus on measurable indicators and output targets. Establish consequences of noncompliance with output targets, or alternatively introduce performance contracts. Develop the budget in a medium-term framework.

		Fully integrate the current and development budget in the context of the medium-term framework.
		Phase in devolution of procurement, payment and payroll processes from the Treasury to the line agencies.
Samoa	In Place: Output budget introduced formally. Integration of current and capital expenditure by output. Medium-term budget framework. Accounting system has been redesigned.	Train central and line agency staff in the new budget system. Begin to broad-band detailed line item input specification after staff training in financial management. Focus on improving measurable indicators and output targets. Introduce corporate planning to link line agency priorities with overall government priorities and policies. Introduce performance contracts, including rewards/sanctions for performance. Improve cost and accounting system.

Full implementation of performance-oriented budgeting holds the potential to improve the productivity of public expenditure in the PMCs, but it is a very complex undertaking. To be successful, both central and line agency managers must acquire resource management skills, and there must be major improvements in the cost accounting systems. If resource management is devolved *before* these conditions are met, productivity could decline. It also needs to be an integral part of a broader program of public management reform, which encourages a culture of performance. Changing budget rules alone will do little to improve performance, and may simply be disruptive. If government intends to outsource, staff capacity in procurement and contract management capacity often requires strengthening.

Staff in both Samoa and Kiribati require more training to understand the new system, much less implement it. In Kiribati, lack of knowledge about costs led to a 30 percent increase in recurrent expenditure in the first year of the performance budget, rather than a hoped-for reduction. Also, staff found it difficult to quantify outputs or measure performance. When corrective action became necessary, the process of implementing performance budgeting became little more than a formality. In Fiji, the budget is unified in the sense that budgeted programs and activities include both recurrent and capital components. Despite this, low public investment expenditure persists, in part because overall expenditure must be restrained, and in part because managers lack autonomy to make personnel decisions, and staff lack the skills to develop "bankable" investment projects.

In Fiji, although current and development expenditure have been integrated within programs and activities, so far this has not triggered a needed increase in public investments, even in core areas. There are several problems: lack of capacity to formulate and prepare projects, lack of flexibility in personnel management, and a tight overall budget constraint.

For PMCs as a whole, strengthening the local evaluation and monitoring capacity for policies, programs and projects will enhance the longer-term prospects because good policies and practices are homegrown rather than externally imposed. It would also ensure that local circumstances are incorporated in policies and projects.

If the investment component of a development activity creates an unsustainable burden on future recurrent expenditure, the investment should be scaled back, and the recurrent component of the activity should be re-evaluated and possibly scaled back, until a sustainable combination of recurrent and development expenditure is reached. Fiji is the only PMC which includes the estimated future recurrent cost of investment in its forward budget. However, any positive effects this might have had on the budget have been masked by recent cuts in operations and maintenance caused by other factors.

To improve the quality of investments included in the budget under the traditional budget system or in a stage of adopting a performance-oriented system, PMCs should institute a three-year rolling PSIP. At a minimum, governments should compile core area projects in a PSIP, and require that all core area projects included in the annual budget must come from the PSIP. This would provide time to analyze and assess projects before they are included in the annual budget. Samoa has recently adopted this model for the PSIP in its three-year Forward Estimate Framework. Since both

central and line agencies lack the skills to do this, improving the quality of projects would require significant training and external technical assistance.

All public investment activities included in the budget should be strictly derived from government policies and priorities. PMC governments need to ensure that the spending agencies' investment proposals are justified by priorities and current activities, and that they are well prepared technically and financially sound. A quality check is essential because line agency staff in virtually all of the countries, as well as agency staff in some of the countries, lack skills to prepare, justify and appraise projects.

AID EFFECTIVENESS. The economies of Pacific Islands are heavily dependent on foreign aid which comprises a large proportion of GDP in most Pacific Island economies. Preferential market access provides additional support. The state dominates the economy, as it must allocate resources to manage, implement and maintain aid-funded projects. Foreign aid can also work against reforms because it provides a comfortable cushion *against* the sharp reform pressures that result from economic adversity. Aid has not always been effective in creating a good growth performance. Major issues to be clarified are: the level of aid, the composition of aid programs, local evaluation, implementation and monitoring capacity, coordination of aid proposals and donor coordination.

This perspective suggests that current aid level increases would be counter-productive unless there were significant changes in its composition and mode of delivery. The Asian Development Bank's current strategy for the Pacific (ADB 1996) recognizes this. Their strategy suggests that any interventions involve significant policy reform or capacity building and address key factors contributing to economic growth.

Other donors can complement this strategy by supporting and developing government functions that adhere to the economic and social fundamentals. Institutional reforms to improve governance, define and protect property rights and liberalize foreign investment are priorities. Funding adjustment programs linked to public sector reform is also important.

The coordination capacity of PMCs is generally very weak and donor coordination is also not very effective. All departments in PMCs need a clear understanding of resource availability and the government's development strategy. Programs need to be prioritized within a sound economic framework and PMCs must develop their own capacity to set priorities and communicate them to donors. Aid would be efficiently used and distortion of domestic policies minimized if government's expenditure programs enabled the government to invite donors to identify and fund sections of the program which may be of interest to them.[4]

Countries with more limited capacity should limit priority development sectors and manage the coordination process to improve aid effectiveness.

Overall, budget reform can be a central element in a broader set of measures aimed at making the government more performance-oriented. In short, the budget can do a great deal to improve performance, but cannot alone bring about change. It needs to be supported by sustained top level commitment backed up by training and technical assistance to strengthening technical and management capacity. To achieve PMC governments' objectives of re-orienting inter and intra-sectoral allocations of expenditures and implementing the comprehensive reform programs many states have adopted, policy planning and budgeting need to be closely linked. Critical to the outcome will be the adoption and development of medium-term expenditure frameworks.

---

4 See Siwatibau (1997, p. 62).

Chart 4.1: Aid per Capita in 107 Low and Middle Income Countries [a]

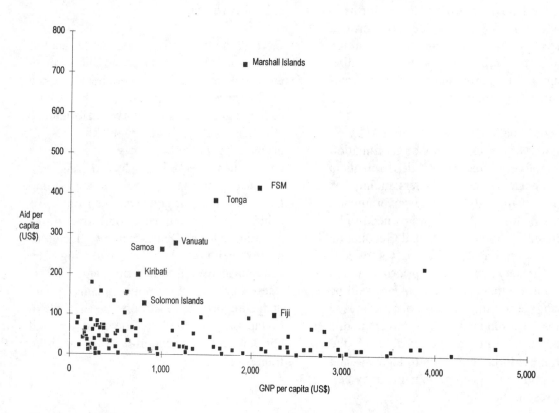

a   The aid per capita figure is based on the level of aid in 1994. The estimates of GNP per capita are mostly for 1994 and are derived
     using the Atlas method (except for the FSM and the Marshall Islands which are GDP per capita).

Sources: World Bank 1997a, World Bank 1996b, AusAID 1997.

COUNTRY PROFILES

COUNTRY PROFILES

FIJI

Population:	**803,000 (1996)**
GDP:	**US$2,126 million (1996)**
GNP Per Capita:	**US$2,470 (1996)**

Introduction

With a population of 803,000 and a GNP per capita of US$2,470 in 1996, Fiji is the most developed of the Pacific Island economies. The country is endowed with abundant natural resources, including timber, minerals, and fisheries resources. Tourism and sugar have been the mainstay of the economy with garment manufacturing emerging as a significant new industry. Fiji has achieved a high level of human resource development as reflected in a life expectancy of 72 years, infant mortality of 22 per thousand, and literacy over 90 percent. However, economic performance during the recent past has been rather poor as elaborated below.

Recent Economic Developments

Following the political events of 1987 and the consequent economic setback, the Fiji Government embarked on implementing a comprehensive set of stabilization and structural reform measures aimed at restoring macroeconomic stability and improving the long-term growth prospects of the economy. While the initial economic response to the program was favorable (GDP grew by over 8 percent during 1989-90), delayed and mixed implementation of key structural elements of the reform program led to a generally disappointing growth performance during the early 1990s. Economic growth turned negative in 1991, and, for the period 1991-95 as a whole, averaged only 2.5 percent. A combination of factors, principally the delay in constitutional reform to ensure an equitable representation of the ethnic groups, the delay in extending the agricultural land leases due to expire shortly, and the slowness in implementing the remaining structural reforms have led to depressed investment levels. At 12 percent of GDP in recent years, total investment is about half the level attained during the early 1980s. This, in turn, has contributed to low economic growth. The new constitution which came into effect in July 1998 is a major achievement and will set a better political platform for future economic growth for Fiji. However, the favorable impact of the new constitution on the economy has yet to be fully realized.

During 1994-95, significant progress was made in maintaining macroeconomic stability: real GDP increased by 3.9 percent in 1994 reflecting strong performance in the sugar and tourism sectors, but slowed considerably to 2.1 percent in 1995, as weather-related factors depressed agricultural output, particularly sugar production. The fiscal deficit reflected greater public sector wage restraint, a decline in cyclone rehabilitation expenditures in 1993, as well as an improvement in VAT compliance and collection as it narrowed considerably to 1.5

percent of GDP in 1994, down from 3.4 percent of GDP a year earlier. A marginal deficit equivalent to 0.5 percent of GDP was recorded in 1995, owing to the strong expansion in income tax receipts and in part due to slow implementation of public investment projects. Consumer inflation decelerated to under 1 percent in 1994, down from over 5 percent in 1993, and remained low in 1995 as credit policies were tightened.

In 1996, real output growth recovered to an estimated 3 percent, boosted by favorable developments in the tourism and sugar sectors. Inflation rose to 3 percent, and the fiscal balance deteriorated considerably, reaching a deficit equivalent to 4.7 percent of GDP (at market prices) by year's end. This deterioration largely stemmed from transfer payments to State-guaranteed depositors of the National Bank of Fiji (NBF), which became insolvent. To address the insolvency crisis, the Government announced a major restructuring effort in mid-1996 designed to streamline the operations of the bank at a cost of about F$200 million (7 percent of GDP). The rising level of public debt (at 40.7 percent of GDP in 1996 or 63.5 percent of GDP including the domestic debt of public enterprises) has also compounded Fiji's fiscal problems.

FIJI: KEY MACRO INDICATORS, 1992-96

	1992	1993	1994	1995	1996
Indicator Levels (US$ million)					
GDP (at current prices)	1541	1640	1811	1999	2126
Govt. Revenues	401	424	477	523	530
Govt. Expenditures	447	481	503	520	636
Govt. Budget Deficit (-)	-46	-57	-26	3	-106
Exports (fob)	349	368	485	520	641
Imports (fob)	539	653	721	761	838
Current Account Balance (after grants)	10	-84	-69	-26	67
Gross Reserves	320	271	275	348	427
Macro Balances (% GDP)					
Budget Deficit (-)	-3.0	-3.4	-1.5	-0.5	-4.7
External Current Account Balance	0.7	-5.1	-3.8	-1.3	3.1
Foreign Public Debt	14.7	12.2	10.1	8.7	7.6
Domestic Public Debt (Central Govt.)	27.5	29.0	29.9	29.4	33.0
Memo Items (% p.a.)					
GDP growth (1989 factor cost)	4.9	2.2	3.9	2.1	3.1
Consumer Inflation (%)	4.9	5.2	0.6	2.2	3.1
Terms of Trade (1990=100)	97.5	100.2	102.3	102.3	99.7
Reserves (mo. imports, fob)	7.1	5.0	4.6	5.5	6.1

Source: IMF Staff Reports, 08/96; Data provided by Fiji authorities.

Despite strong tourist activity in the first half of the year, economic performance in 1997 was weak as domestic demand remained sluggish. Uncertainties in the sugar sector continued to weaken business confidence. Weak international commodity prices, particularly for gold, as well as depressed sugar output as a result of adverse weather, also negatively impacted economic performance. Real GDP growth was estimated at -1.8 percent for the year. Consumer inflation eased to under 2 percent by the middle of the year from a high of over 4 percent during the early months of the year. Inflationary pressures remained low for the rest of the year with continued exchange rate stability and low inflation in Fiji's trading partners.

Key Policy Issues

Resolving the NBF Financial Crisis. The losses of the NBF have been larger than anticipated. Consequently, government expenditures, the fiscal deficit, and public debt levels have risen significantly above originally targeted levels for both 1996 and 1997. A successful resolution of the financial crisis without endangering macroeconomic stability will be essential for the revival of investor confidence.

Resolving Policy Uncertainty. Although there have been recent constitutional reforms, the issue of expiration of land leases continues to cloud the economic environment. A speedy resolution of the uncertainty surrounding agricultural land leases, particularly sugarcane land leases, are of priority for economic and social development.

Restoring Investment. Economic growth in Fiji remains at around 2.5 percent per year, reflecting in large part the low investment rate in the economy of about 12 to 14 percent of GDP. Although recent constitutional reforms have been an important step forward, the investment climate continues to be dampened by uncertainty surrounding the future of land leases expiring in the short term, procedural constraints, and public service attitudes which regulate rather than facilitate private sector development. As long as these concerns persist, policy reforms directed at stimulating investment will have limited impact. Growth prospects will remain poor unless there is a stronger commitment to stable and sound social and economic policies.

Curbing Public Sector Wage Growth. Central government current expenditures continue to be disproportionately large, amounting to 85 to 90 percent of total expenditure, while development expenditures are low and declining. The public sector wage bill currently accounts for almost half of recurrent expenditures, while funds for purchases of goods and services, and operations and maintenance have been curtailed, with the sharpest cuts concentrated in operations and maintenance. These large imbalances in aggregate expenditure point to a problem of low development effectiveness, including low productivity of government workers, insufficient investment to provide essential support for private sector-led growth, and inadequate provision for maintenance and operation of existing government assets, with consequent reduction in the return to government investment. The present strategy to reach a balanced budget by the year 2000 through yearly reductions in expenditures of non-core ministries is likely to result in increased inefficiencies if expenditure cuts are made in nonwage recurrent and development outlays. Controlling civil service wage levels and the size of the public wage bill is key to influencing the overall competitiveness of the economy as well as fiscal and macroeconomic stability.

Public Enterprise Reform and Privatization. Fiji has taken some important steps in public sector reform in three areas: (a) civil service reform which involves a movement towards contract employment and greater flexibility in hiring and firing of staff; (b) public enterprise reforms through corporatization as a first step; and (c) financial management reform, essentially on planning and budgeting. While there is a comprehensive public enterprise reform program in place, some problems persist, including implementation capacity and adjustment issues for workers.

Restructuring Sugar. With the gradual erosion of preferential sugar prices, Fiji will no longer be able to enjoy the benefits from the subsidized sugar prices it currently receives under the Sugar Protocol of the Lomé Convention. Uncertainty in the sugar industry has also been compounded in recent years by the finalization of the review of land leases under ALTA. As farmers have been uncertain about their future, they have been hesitant to invest in their farms in the fear that their leases may not be renewed. Another direct consequence of this uncertainty has been the increasing reluctance of lending institutions to lend money to farmers for capital investment. Given the importance of the sugar subsector in the Fiji economy, the need to resolve the issue is critical. Recent efforts to improve efficiency in the industry include an agreement to pay sugar prices in line with quality rather than quantity of cane. The Fiji Sugar Commission is also seeking government funding of F$125 million over five years to upgrade milling and transport infrastructure so as to improve productivity.

Government Objectives and Policies: Promoting Economic and Social Well-being of Fijians

The Government's priority goals over the next two years are detailed in the document *"Preparing for the 1997 Budget, Action Now, April, 1996."* These are summarized as follows: (i) sustained real economic growth to ensure poverty alleviation; (ii) a sustainable government financial position, preferably with a balanced budget and manageable debt levels; (iii) growing levels of employment (formal and informal) in the economy intended to ensure employment rates of at least 95 percent of the total labor force; (iv) improvements in the well-being of rural communities with rural incomes increasing to an average of at least F$175 per week and reductions in poverty levels to levels below those established in the 1990/91 Household Income and Expenditure Survey; (v) improving health for Fiji's population as indicated by life expectancy at birth of at least 75 years by 2000; and (iv) continuing improvements in the level of education of Fiji's people to a point where the combination of primary and secondary school enrollment ratios in the country are at least 88 percent. To achieve these objectives, the Government intends to move quickly in the following policy areas: (i) improve operational efficiency and reduce the size of government; (ii) secure property rights for every citizen; (iii) improve the operation of domestic markets; and (iv) broaden external trading opportunities.

KIRIBATI

Population:	**81,600 (1996)**
GDP:	**US$55 million (1996)**
GNP Per Capita:	**US$870 (1996)**

Introduction

With a GNP per capita of US$870 in 1996, Kiribati is in the category of low income countries. The bulk of the population is employed in the subsistence sector with formal employment being dominated by the public sector, which accounts for 95 percent of gross investment and almost half of GDP. The private sector is small and underdeveloped. Although the natural environment and infertile soil constrain agricultural development, the nation possesses abundant ocean resources, principally fish, seaweed, and manganese. Kiribati also obtains large inflows of income from abroad in the form of earnings from the Revenue Equalization Reserve Fund (RERF), fishing licenses issued to foreign fleets, and remittances from natives working overseas in shipping and mining. Official development assistance is also an important element of the economy, having financed a large public sector and contributed to a relatively underdeveloped private sector.

Recent Economic Developments

Since its independence in 1979, Kiribati has achieved a solid record of financial stability, notwithstanding a limited range of economic assets. This is reflected in overall budget surpluses in several years, relatively small deficits in other years, and a steady rise in external reserves to around nine years of import cover. However, Kiribati's development record has been rather poor. While real GDP growth per capita has been negative for many years, there has been some social progress, as indicated by the increase in life expectancy from 51 years in the late 1970s to 57 years in 1985-90, and a decline in the infant mortality rate from 82 to 65 per 1,000 over the same period, as well as an improvement in the primary school enrollment rate from 76 percent to 85 percent for the six to nine year cohort. These results reflect the Government's emphasis on health and education expenditures over the years. But these social indicators compare unfavorably with those achieved by other Pacific Island Countries.

After 1980, when mining operations ceased to be the main economic activity, economic growth has been slow and erratic, reflecting the vulnerability of the country's main export commodities (copra and marine products) to price and environmental shocks. After negative real per capita growth rates during 1979-94, real GDP grew by an estimated 3 percent in 1995, largely driven by expansionary fiscal policies. Real GDP growth is estimated to be less than 2 percent in 1996, reflecting a decline in copra production and fishing activities. Inflation has remained low at 4 percent in 1995, and negligible in 1996, owing to the use of the Australian dollar as national currency, and resistance to price increases for goods and services provided by public enterprises.

KIRIBATI: KEY MACRO INDICATORS, 1992-96

	1992	1993	1994	1995	1996
Indicator Levels (US$ million)					
GDP (at current prices)	33.7	32.8	39.9	47.8	54.6
Govt. Revenues	51.4	46.9	47.9	50.9	43.8
Govt. Expenditures	39.9	32.6	38.0	44.5	47.7
Govt. Budget Deficit (-)	11.5	14.2	9.9	6.4	-3.9
Exports (fob)	4.8	3.5	5.3	7.4	5.8
Imports (fob)	37.1	27.8	26.4	35.2	37.4
Current Account Balance (after grants)	3.5	5.2	13.0	5.3	-2.3
Gross Reserves	223	266	283	308	330
Macro Balances (% GDP)					
Budget Deficit (-)	34.2	43.1	24.6	13.2	-7.2
External Current Account Balance	10.5	15.7	32.5	11.0	-4.3
Memo Items (% p.a.)					
GDP growth	-1.6	1.0	1.7	3.3	1.9
Consumer Inflation (%)	4.0	6.1	5.3	3.6	-0.6
Reserves (yr. imports, fob)	6.4	9.6	10.1	8.7	8.7

Source: IMF Staff Reports, 05/97.

In 1997, growth is estimated to be zero or negative as a result of reduced government expenditures and a 45 percent fall in copra production.   Inflation rose to 2.2 percent, and the underlying budget balance (excluding earnings on external assets) registered a significant surplus reflecting abnormally high fishing license fees. To sustain growth, more concrete policies and actions are needed to encourage the development of the private sector and reduce the size of the public sector.

Key Development Issues

Achieving Higher Sustainable Growth. While an expansionary fiscal stance will stimulate the economy, albeit temporarily, there is an urgent need for economic restructuring to re-orient   the economy toward private sector–led growth.   The Government needs to pursue a more vibrant higher growth development strategy based on a progressive right-sizing of the public sector, and focus resources on core functions of government to gradually allow an increasing role for the private sector, church groups, non-government organiza-ions and other stakeholders in the economy. The role of the private sector needs to be enhanced through improvements in the trade and tax regimes and the regulatory environment.

Improving Effectiveness of Government Expenditure. A restructuring of government to emphasize its core functions should not only aim at shifting aggregate expenditures toward the core sectors of government, but should also focus on changes in expenditure within sectors to improve the efficiency of expenditure and support government objectives. Non–wage expenditures, especially operations and maintenance, should receive greater priority.

Public Sector Reform. Up to late 1994, government policy had emphasized the importance of privatizing public enterprises which dominate activity in virtually all sectors of the economy. Until the early 1990s, government subsidies to the enterprises were progressively reduced to encourage increased efficiency. However, little progress was made in truly commercializing them. As most of the enterprises continued to perform poorly without significant changes in management and practices, they were also a drain on the budget, both in terms of revenue forgone and in terms of direct and indirect government support such as subsidies, net lending and government guarantees for bank overdrafts. The Government which assumed office in late 1994 changed the divestment strategy to one of truly commercializing operations of most public enterprises while retaining them in the public sector. Divestment was considered to be a possibility at a later stage. While in 1995, two public enterprises were liquidated and successor companies were established (also fully government–owned) in effect the Government has maintained control of most of the public enterprises through their boards and supervising ministries. So far there has been little success in truly commercializing any of the public enterprise operations, although feasibility studies of commercializing the postal operations and the philatelic office are being carried out. In view of the many years of unsuccessfully commercializing the public enterprises, and considering the high cost to both the budget and the economy of maintaining inefficient enterprises, the Government should reconsider its strategy and undertake a program of divestment to let the market produce more efficient companies.

FEDERATED STATES OF MICRONESIA

Population:	**110,000 (1996)**
GDP:	**US$226 million (1996)**
GNP Per Capita:	**US$2,050 (1996)**

Introduction

The Federated States of Micronesia has a narrow production base comprising primarily subsistence farming, and reef and deep-sea fishing. Manufacturing and other industrial activities constitute only a very small component of GDP. The dominant sector and the largest employer is the public sector, accounting for over 75 percent of GDP. As a small island economy, development is constrained by the dispersal of the land mass, shortages of skilled labor, high wages and remoteness from markets. Social development indicators lag behind those of other Pacific Island countries, despite a comparatively high per capita income estimated at around US$2,050 in 1996.

Recent Economic Developments

Economic performance has been poor in recent years, characterized by low real output growth, fiscal deficits and large external debt. Moreover, the country faces a difficult adjustment period over the next several years as U.S. Compact assistance is scheduled to be eliminated by 2001. Also, because of the limited role of monetary policy due to the use of the U.S. dollar as legal tender, the burden of adjustment must fall on fiscal policy.

Real GDP grew by an average of only 1 percent per year during 1994-96, substantially lower than an estimated growth of nearly 6 percent attained in 1993, when fishing activity increased considerably and several major public investment projects were completed. The disappointing performance of economic activity in recent years is largely attributable to sluggish activity in tourism, fisheries and agriculture, particularly copra, the main cash crop, owing in part to an aging tree stock. The poor state of public finances has also adversely affected business activity in recent years. Consumer inflation, based on price trends in the United States and Marshall Islands because of the lack of compilation of price indexes in the country, remained moderate at around 4 percent per year during 1994-96, down slightly from rates recorded during the previous two years.

The national government continues to subsidize copra production through the Coconut Development Authority, which handles the purchase and export of copra. Some diversification of agricultural production has occurred into pepper, bananas, betel nuts, and citrus products. Tourism activity continues to be limited to niche markets, including ecotourism and shipwreck diving in the Chuuk and Yap states. Growth remains hampered by the lack of infrastructure and distance from potential markets, while the development of resorts is hindered by the complex land tenure system and environmental concerns. Activity in the garment sector has not expanded in recent years. Both the national and state governments recognize the potential role of foreign investment in expanding and diversifying the productive base. A number of incentives are available to attract foreign direct investment, including duty-free access to the U.S. market for most products. Foreign direct investment exemptions are offered only for exports. There are no (tax) exemptions from income tax, gross revenue taxes, and import duties. The FSM intends to consider the introduction of a broad-based consumption tax with excises on selected items. However, the investment approval process is cumbersome as both the national and state governments must ratify each project. The weak legal infrastructure and limitations on land ownership and use also constitute impediments to potential investors.

The consolidated budgetary position of the government has remained weak despite lower capital spending. Although the overall consolidated fiscal position of the Government swung from a deficit of 0.5 percent of GDP in 1993/94 to a surplus of 1.6 percent of GDP in 1994/95, an estimated US$17 million in domestic payments arrears were accumulated, particularly by the state government of Chuuk. In addition, domestic revenues fell and progress in reducing current expenditure was limited. In 1995/96, the consolidated budget deficit was estimated at 2 percent of GDP, a substantial deterioration from the two preceding years. The formulation of a consistent national fiscal policy continues to be hindered by the structure of relations between the national and state authorities. While the national government has the responsibility for policy coordination, the state authorities have a high degree of autonomy in the implementation of budgetary policies. In recent months, though, there has been a proposal to form an FSM-wide Tax Authority to consolidate the national, state and local tax administration efforts.

FSM: KEY MACRO INDICATORS, 1991/92-95/96

	1991/92	1992/93	1993/94	1994/95	1995/96
Indicator Levels (US$ million)					
GDP (at current prices)	174.1	195.0	205.5	215.8	226.4
Govt. Revenues	155.5	162.7	166.2	172.5	169.4
Govt. Expenditures	164.8	169.0	167.3	169.1	173.4
Govt. Budget Deficit (-)	-9.3	-6.3	-1.1	3.4	-4.0
Exports (fob)	21.0	28.1	66.3	69.6	73.1
Imports (fob)	123.4	137.2	160.0	164.5	167.6
Current Account Balance (after grants)	2.3	-2.1	13.4	15.4	8.6
Gross Reserves a/	65.1	68.0	50.2	40.0	30.8
Macro Balances (% GDP)					
Budget Deficit (-)	-5.3	-3.3	-0.6	1.6	-1.8
External Current Account Balance	1.3	-1.1	6.5	7.1	3.8
Foreign Public Debt	66.6	70.1	62.7	55.4	49.6
Memo Items (% p.a.)					
GDP growth	-1.2	5.7	1.4	1.0	1.0
Consumer Inflation (%)	5.0	6.0	4.0	4.0	4.0
Terms of Trade (% change)					
Reserves (mo. imports, fob)	6.3	5.9	3.8	2.9	2.2

a/ Government financial holdings.

Source: IMF Staff Reports, 07/96.

Corresponding to the weak fiscal position, the external current account deficit (excluding grants) has remained high at around 50 percent of GDP in recent years despite higher fish exports. The deficit is estimated to have declined only marginally to 47 percent of GDP in 1995/96. External debt, comprising government and government-guaranteed debt continues to be high. At the end of the 1994/95 fiscal year, external debt outstanding stood at 55 percent of GDP, with substantial amounts on commercial terms. External debt service amounted to the equivalent of 18 percent of exports of goods and services. Government financial holdings had been progressively drawn down to less than three months of imports, about half the ratio attained three years before. At the end of the 1995/96 fiscal year, government cash reserves were estimated to have dropped further to the equivalent of two months of imports.

Government Objectives and Policies

Consistent with IMF recommendations, the Government has formulated a structural reform program which has been under implementation since 1995. The program aims at restoring macroeconomic stability and promoting sustainable growth and external viability in the post-Compact era. The proposed strategy of promoting private sector activity and downsizing of the public sector was endorsed by the national economic summit held in November 1995, and by the donor community during the first Consultative Group meeting organized by the Asian Development Bank in December 1995. Considerable progress has been made under the reform program during the past two years, particularly the recent National Government Restructuring that has contributed to downsizing of the public sector, a major goal of the economic reform effort. In the area of private sector development, foreign investment policy has been simplified through the enactment of a new Foreign Investment Act aimed at streamlining the foreign investment approval process, devolving most discretionary powers to the states and creating a more competitive environment for the attraction of foreign investment. There were some reforms made to the taxation system as well, notably the enactment of a new Customs Act of 1997, designed to increase customs revenues appreciably in the future. Good progress has also been made in financial sector reform, with IMF technical assistance, including some liberalization in interest rates.

Key Development Issues

Strengthening Public Finances. While the Government has responded in the past to declining external grants partly by resorting to external commercial borrowing against future Compact funds, as well drawdown of government cash holdings, the strategy is clearly not sustainable. As the Compact assistance is being phased out, there is an urgent need for wide-ranging fiscal adjustment measures including increased domestic resource mobilization and reduced public expenditures to curb consumption and lessen dependence on imports.

Promoting Private Sector Growth. Private sector development of agriculture, fisheries and tourism is crucial to promoting external viability. Growth of the private sector would require the upgrading of labor skills, a consistent regulatory framework, reform of the land tenure system, continued simplification of foreign investment policy, a more efficient financial system as well as further reforms to the taxation system. To support expansion of the productive base, including manufacturing and the tourist sector, adequate infrastructure and services are needed. The investment program would need to focus on development of social and economic infrastructure to support private sector activity. A comprehensive reform of the education system is also essential to provide education and skills training more relevant to the needs of the country.

MARSHALL ISLANDS

Population:	**58,000 (1996)**
GDP:	**US$108 million (1996)**
GNP Per Capita:	**US$1,860 (1996)**

Introduction

The Marshall Islands has a narrow production base consisting primarily of coconut harvesting and processing, subsistence farming and deep sea fishing. The government sector dominates the economy, accounting for almost half of formal employment. As a small island economy, economic growth is constrained by the dispersal of atolls, shortages of skilled labor, high wages and remoteness from markets. Social development indicators lag behind those of other Pacific Island countries, despite a comparatively high per capita income estimated at around US$1,860 in 1996.

Recent Economic Developments

Economic performance has been disappointing in recent years, characterized by low real output growth, unsustainable fiscal deficits, a weak balance of payments and large external debts. The Government has exhausted its financial holdings and borrowing capacity. The public sector remains overstaffed and inefficient, while there are only few job opportunities in the private sector. The country is now in the process of adjusting to the decline of assistance from the U.S. under the Compact of Free Association, which requires substantial fiscal adjustment. Reform programs have been designed and initial measures have been taken which have already led to improvements in the fiscal position. However, there remains an urgent need to continue the implementation of the required reforms in order to reach sustainable and self-reliant growth before 2001 when Compact assistance will terminate.

Real GDP growth averaged less than 3 percent per year during the early 1990s. However, increased foreign investment in fisheries as well as increased activity in the copra industry boosted economic growth to nearly 4 percent in 1995. Real output is estimated to have declined by nearly 3 percent in 1996, reflecting mainly recessionary conditions in the fishing industry as foreign investment declined, as well as reduced copra output in response to unfavorable prices. Consumer inflation rose to 7 percent in 1995, up from 5 percent in 1993. This reflected mainly higher prices for household supplies and clothing on account of reduced competition in the retail sector as major retail outlet closed. Inflationary pressures are estimated to have moderated to 4 percent in 1996.

The fiscal deficit was estimated at 2 percent of GDP in 1995/96, substantially down from an average of 13 percent of GDP recorded during the previous three years when capital expenditures expanded considerably on account of increased spending on education, infrastructure and other public investment projects. Recurrent expenditures, particularly the wage and salary bill, were also high during the period as controls on recruitment were not strictly enforced. The improvement in the budgetary situation for the 1995/96 fiscal year was largely attributable to revenue-raising measures and cuts in current spending introduced in a supplementary budget during March 1996. Development expenditures were also lower in 1996 despite construction of a government-owned hotel in that year.

The deficits of the early 1990s, financed largely by borrowing against future Compact revenues, have led to rising external debt and debt service levels as well as exhaustion of government financial holdings. At the end of the 1994/95 fiscal year, external debt outstanding, mostly on commercial terms, stood at 138 percent of GDP, while the debt service ratio amounted to 42 percent of exports of goods and services during the year. External debt outstanding is estimated to have declined to 118 percent of GDP in 1995/96 as government refrained from new commercial borrowing; however, the debt service burden remained high. The external current account deficit (excluding grants), which has been unusually large at around 60 percent of GDP, reflecting strong import demand and large interest payments, declined to 50 percent of GDP in 1996 as import demand weakened.

MARSHALL ISLANDS: KEY MACRO INDICATORS, 1991/92-95/96

	1991/92	1992/93	1993/94	1994/95	1995/96
Indicator Levels (US$ million)					
GDP (at current prices)	77.8	85.2	92.7	102.6	108.4
Govt. Revenues	67.2	72.9	70.9	76.7	74.9
Govt. Expenditures	87.7	84.9	83.4	89.4	76.8
Govt. Budget Deficit (-)	-20.5	-12.0	-12.5	-12.7	-1.9
Exports (fob)	9.6	7.9	14.8	17.0	17.5
Imports (cif)	60.5	61.3	68.1	73.9	71.8
Current Account Balance (after grants)	-0.2	-1.0	0.0	-6.2	1.3
Gross Reserves a/	29.3	28.9	37.9	12.9	0.4
Macro Balances (% GDP)					
Budget Deficit (-)	-26.3	-14.1	-13.5	-12.4	-1.8
External Current Account Balance	-0.3	-1.2	0.0	-6.0	1.2
Foreign Public Debt	138.2	143.5	165.0	137.7	118.2
Memo Items (% p.a.)					
GDP growth	0.1	4.1	2.8	3.7	-2.5
Consumer Inflation (%)	10.3	5.0	5.6	7.3	4.0
Reserves (mo. imports, cif)	5.8	5.7	6.7	2.1	0.1

a/ Government financial holdings.
Source: IMF Staff Reports, 07/96.

Government Objectives and Policies

The Marshall Islands faces an extremely difficult adjustment period over the next several years because of the phased reduction of the United States Compact assistance and its scheduled elimination in 2000/01. In recognition of the daunting task ahead, the Government has prepared a Policy Reform Program (PRP), a comprehensive reform program, aimed at restoring macroeconomic stability, downsizing the public sector and promoting private sector growth. Donors endorsed the reform program during the first Consultative Group Meeting held in December 1995 under the sponsorship of the Asian Development Bank. Under the Public

Sector Reform Program, the main component of the PRP, considerable progress has been made since its adoption in 1996, albeit there has been some slippage in timetables for meeting specific conditions; also, the pace of reform has slowed. The main progress made includes a 25 percent reduction in civil service staff since January 1996; other important reform measures announced in the FY98 budget include continued reduction in staff of the public service to meet agreed targets, termination of subsidies to Air Marshall Islands and continued public sector wage freeze, a second tranche release condition to the ADB program loan. Also notable is the rationalization of the tariff structure during FY96, simplification of the payments system and amalgamation of ministries to minimize duplication of services and reduce the range of services provided by the Government. Various other reforms are also at different stages of implementation, including the introduction of a performance-based budgeting system, the introduction of a broad-based consumption tax (value added tax) as well as measures to privatize public enterprises.

Key Development Issues

Promoting a Higher and Sustainable Level of Growth. In view of declining per capita real output, there is an urgent need to intensify implementation efforts under the reform program to achieve a higher and sustainable real output growth. U.S. financial assistance provided under the Compact and intended to provide the necessary resources to create the infrastructure and institutions required for the Marshall Islands to function as a fully independent state has met with little success. Clearly, past policy failures need to be addressed and advantage taken of future aid to improve economic performance.

Promoting Private Sector Growth. In line with the Government's reform program, there is the need for a massive fiscal adjustment, much of it front-loaded, to generate overall fiscal surpluses necessary to meet debt service obligations and rebuild government financial holdings. This strategy should help to secure a significant fall in the external current account deficit through a steady increase in public sector savings, while permitting a higher investment necessary to support private sector development. Growth of the private sector would require a more efficient financial system, a consistent regulatory framework, reform of the land tenure system, and simplification of foreign investment policy. To support expansion of the productive base, including manufacturing and the tourist sector, adequate infrastructure and services are needed. The investment program would need to focus on development of social and economic infrastructure to support private sector activity. Private sector development should focus more on providing support for small entrepreneurs and traders.

Other Reform Measures. As the Compact assistance is being phased out, other fiscal adjustment measures should include increased domestic resource mobilization and reduced public expenditures to curb consumption and lessen dependence on imports. Also requiring attention is the downsizing of the public sector workforce, reduction in wages, amalgamation of Ministries and a continued reduction in subsidies to public enterprises, particularly Air Marshall Islands. There is also the need to discontinue and further contract out a number of functions currently undertaken by the Government.

REPUBLIC OF PALAU

Population: **18,125 (1996) Est.**

GDP: **US$145 million (1996)**

GDP Per Capita: **US$8,000 (1996)**

Introduction

The Republic of Palau became a member of the IMF and World Bank Group effective December 16, 1997. The country, consisting of more than 200 islands, was part of the Trust Territory of the Pacific administered by the United States following World War II, until it became a self-governing republic in 1980. In October 1994, a Compact of Free Association signed with the United States in 1982 (later amended in 1986) became effective, rendering the Republic of Palau a sovereign state. Under the terms of the Compact, the United States agreed to provide economic assistance and benefits to Palau over a 15-year period in the amount of US$500 million, adjusted for inflation.

Besides a large public sector, the economy has a narrow production base, consisting primarily of fishing and tourism, albeit in recent years the production base has benefited from foreign direct investment inflows as well as foreign labor. The services sector dominates the economy, accounting for around 80 percent of GDP in 1996. The industrial sector, rather small, constituted 11 percent of GDP while agriculture (including fisheries) and the subsistence sector (comprising subsistence agriculture and inshore fishing) contributed 7 percent and 2 percent of GDP respectively in 1996.

As a small island state, the development constraints faced by Palau are akin to those found in other Pacific Island countries. These include remoteness from major external markets, vulnerability to natural hazards and other natural handicaps, as well as lack of professional skills and poor infrastructure. However, the rich marine resources of Palau, as well as its unspoiled natural beauty, offer the country opportunities for further growth and development. The population is highly urbanized with easy access to basic services and employment. The Government continues to be the largest employer, although its share of total employment declined to 30 percent in 1995, down from 38 percent in 1990, while the share of other service sectors increased from 37 percent to 46 percent over the same period.

Recent Economic Developments

The economy is estimated to have grown substantially after independence in 1994 largely due to strong tourist arrivals as well as the inflow of Compact funds which has fueled strong growth in consumption activity over time. At over 60,000 visitors in 1996, tourist and business arrivals was about three and a half times the country's population during that year. Nominal GDP expanded at an average rate of nearly 13 percent per year over the 1991/92 to 1995/96 period notwithstanding moderate declines during the early 1990s when fishcatch dropped and construction activity stalled, in part due to weak project implementation capacity. Although no systematic price information is currently available, consumer price inflation is considered to have increased during 1990-96 as import prices in the U.S. its main trading partner, rose and the U.S. dollar depreciated over the period, raising import prices of non-US sourced goods.

REPUBLIC OF PALAU: KEY MACRO INDICATORS, 1991/92-95/96

	1991/92	1992/93	1993/94	1994/95	1995/96
Indicator Levels (US$ million)					
GDP (at current prices)	82.5	75.9	88.9	117.6	145.1
Govt. Revenues	47.5	49.4	49.6	168.1	67.2
Govt. Expenditures	50.5	46.6	50.4	67.6	75.1
Govt. Budget Deficit (-)	-3.0	2.8	-0.8	100.5	-7.9
Exports (fob)	26.9	17.7	12.6	13.9	14.3
Imports (fob)	38.1	42.2	44.2	60.4	72.4
Current Account Balance (after grants)	16.2	4.8	5.4	71.8	23.3
Macro Balances (% GDP)					
Budget Deficit (-)	-3.6	3.7	-0.9	85.5	-5.4
External Current Account Balance	19.6	6.3	6.1	61.1	16.1
Memo Items (% p.a.)					
Nominal GDP growth	-1.7	-8.0	17.2	32.2	23.4

Source: IMF Staff Report, 07/97.

After averaging a deficit of over 1 percent of GDP during the early 1990s, the overall fiscal balance (including grants), swung into a substantial surplus in the mid-1990s, registering the equivalent of about 91 percent of GDP in 1994/95. The substantial improvement in the budgetary position during 1994/95 largely stemmed from a surge in compact grants which were estimated to have increased nearly five-fold compared to previous years, owing to front-loading. The overall fiscal position shifted into a deficit of about 5.4 percent of GDP in 1995/96 as compact funds declined as scheduled and development expenditures increased sharply as delayed capital projects were implemented. Excluding grants, however, the budgetary position was in substantial deficit during the 1990s and rising. At the end of 1994/95, the fiscal deficit stood at 47 percent of GDP, up 10 percentage points from three years earlier,

before declining slightly to 40 percent of GDP in 1995/96. On an annual average basis, the fiscal deficit (excluding grants) averaged 40 percent of GDP over the 1990-96 period.

The external sector has been characterized by a narrow export base (consisting primarily of fish exports, mainly high-grade fresh tuna), heavy reliance on imports, substantial earnings from tourism and large foreign assistance, mainly U.S. Compact funds. Owing to rising tourism receipts in recent years as well as sizable inflows of compact grants, the external current account has been in surplus, rising to 61 percent of GDP in 1994/95, up from 6 percent of GDP in 1992/93, but dropping off to 16 percent of GDP in 1995/96, the average level attained at the beginning of the 1990s. The unusually large surplus in 1995/96 was mainly accounted for by the front-loading of

Compact grants. The overall external balance, reflecting mainly changes in the financial holdings of the Government (excluding Compact Section 211(f) Trust Fund) has generally been in deficit except in 1995/96, when it recorded a large surplus amounting to US$96 million partly due to a large inflow of grants received for capital improvement. Palau's external reserves, which include unspent Compact funds earmarked for capital improvement projects, as well as the Trust Fund for use in financing future current expenditures of the national government, stood at SDR 163 million (US$234 million) at the end of December 1996, equivalent to about 19 months of total imports of goods and services.

A source of vulnerability to which Palau will have to adjust in recent times is the East Asian financial crisis. With about 85 percent of estimated tourists and business visitors originating from Asian countries, foreign exchange receipts are likely to be adversely affected, leading to a possibly weaker external position.

Government Objectives and Policies

In anticipation of the cessation of U.S. Compact assistance by 2009, the Government approved, in 1996, a National Master Plan which sets forth the framework and policies for the pursuit of sustained economic and social development over a 25-year period. The main long-term development objectives of the Master Plan are summarized as follows: (i) a substantial shift in economic activity from the public sector to the private sector aimed at increasing productivity and efficiency of resource use; (ii) strengthening of Government institutions to improve coordination of decisionmaking processes while, at the same time, reducing the relative

size of government; and (iii) identification of financing strategies, including tax reform, to offset the decline in U.S. assistance over time. Within the framework of the Master Plan, a five-year Development Plan for 1994/95 to 1998/99 was also adopted with specific emphasis on infrastructure and other capital outlays.

Key Development Issues

Developing the Productive Capacity of the Economy. Over the coming years, as Compact funds are programmed to decline, the key challenge facing the Government is to develop the productive capacity of the economy and to make successful transition from a subsistence to a market-based economy. Accordingly, the Government's approved National Master Development Plan that sets forth strategies for the pursuit of sustained economic and social development over a 25-year period, augurs well for the future.

Strengthening Public Finances. The Government's fiscal strategy over the medium term should aim at strengthening the country's financial holdings rather than borrowing against future Compact funds. Toward this end, the Government should adhere to its intentions to pursue wide-ranging fiscal reforms including broadening the existing limited tax base.

Other Issues. In line with the objectives of the Master Plan, there is the need to accelerate private sector development in order to promote external viability. As the Compact assistance is being phased out, other fiscal adjustment measures should include increased domestic resource mobilization and reduced public expenditures to curb consumption and lessen dependence on imports.

SAMOA

Population:	**167,100 (1996)**
GDP:	**US$175 million (1996)**
GNP Per Capita:	**US$1,200 (1996)**

Introduction

With a GNP per capita of US$1,200 in 1996, the Samoan economy has long been characterized by low productivity, low growth and a dominant public sector. About 28 percent of the US$175 million economy (1996 estimate) is in subsistence form. Primary sectors (including subsistence agriculture, forestry and fisheries) account for 40 percent of 1996 GDP, while the secondary sectors (manufacturing, industry and construction), and services sector (excluding government) each for about one-fourth; government services accounted for 11 percent of GDP. The economy is open with total trade (goods and services) accounting for 115 percent of GDP in 1996. The major cash crops are coconut, taro and cocoa.

Recent Economic Developments

Following the adverse economic shocks of the early 1990s when the economy was hit by two severe cyclones, economic performance has improved considerably during the mid-1990s, reflecting a recovery in agricultural production, reconstruction of infrastructure following the cyclones, rebounding of tourism, and a tight fiscal stance. Real GDP increased by about 10 percent in 1995 and by a further 6 percent in 1996 to reach its pre-cyclone level of 1989. With population growth rate of 0.6 percent per year (net of migration), this represents a total of 4.3 percent fall in per capita income between 1989 and 1996.

In spite of the low growth of output, the country now enjoys a healthy international reserve position, a moderate rate of inflation, and a relatively stable exchange rate. Macroeconomic stability has been achieved, inter alia, through sharply shrinking the fiscal deficit, rebuilding private sector confidence, maintaining political stability and continuity in government administration. The fiscal balance swung from a deficit equivalent to 22 percent of GDP in 1992/93 (at the peak of the rehabilitation period) to a surplus of 1.9 percent of GDP in 1995/96, due mainly to the completion of cyclone-related rehabilitation projects, which were financed by concessional borrowing. The Government's overall deficit target for 1996/97 is projected at 3 percent of GDP, to be financed solely by foreign loans. Monetary policy was relaxed during 1995, a time of marked increase in credit. Inflation declined from 18 percent in 1994 to 1 percent in 1995, reflecting improved food supply (including small recovery in taro production), before accelerating to 7.5 percent in 1996; non-food inflation continues to be a relatively modest 3 percent. Gross official reserves have averaged over 6 months of import cover during the past five years.

The return of the Government in April 1996 has stabilized political uncertainties and set the stage for a vigorous implementation of public sector reform and privatization, which the Government initiated in the early 1990s. In spite of favorable social indicators, the economy remains structurally weak and highly dependent on foreign aid remittances from expatriate Samoans.

SAMOA: KEY MACRO INDICATORS, 1992-96

	1992	1993	1994	1995	1996
Indicator Levels (US$ million)					
GDP (at current prices)	119.7	121.3	136.9	155.0	175.3
Govt. Revenues	64.6	71.9	70.3	87.9	103.3
Govt. Expenditures	83.7	98.0	85.3	102.0	100.2
Govt. Budget Deficit (-)	-19.1	-26.1	-15.0	-14.1	3.1
Exports (fob)	5.8	6.4	3.5	8.8	10.1
Imports (cif)	110.1	102.7	80.1	92.2	99.0
Current Account Balance (after grants)	-25.4	-31.0	5.8	9.4	15.6
Gross Reserves	56.9	47.9	47.0	47.8	56.8
Macro Balances (% GDP)					
Budget Deficit (-)	-16.5	-22.0	-11.5	-9.6	1.9
External Current Account Balance (after grants)	-21.2	-25.6	4.2	6.1	8.9
Foreign Public Debt	98.5	159.8	114.6	110.0	95.2
Memo Items (% p.a.)					
GDP growth	-0.2	4.1	-6.5	9.6	5.9
Consumer Inflation (%)	8.5	1.7	18.4	1.0	7.5
Terms of Trade (% change)	6.8	10.5	-18.3	-10.6	-0.1
Reserves (mo. imports, cif)	6.2	5.6	7.0	6.2	6.9

Source: IMF Recent Economic Developments, 03/97; World Bank DRS.

Key Development Issues

Public Sector Reform. The Government has formulated a comprehensive public-sector reform program aimed at improving the efficiency of the public sector and fiscal management. The main elements of the reform strategy include commitments to (i) reduce the relative role of the public sector and withdraw from certain services that could be more efficiently carried out by the private sector; (ii) reform the financial system through the establishment of a performance budgeting framework and the phased devolution of accounting functions to line agencies; and (iii) enhance the management of line agency personnel through the delegation of human resource operational functions to line agencies. The central element of the public sector reform is the implementation of the performance budgeting framework. During 1995-96, performance budgeting was implemented in the Departments of Agriculture, Public Works and Treasury. For the 1996/97 fiscal year, the new framework was extended to all departments. The new focus on outputs necessitated the integration of the old recurrent and development budgets, and accounting systems were recast to account for the costs incurred in production of outputs. Outputs are classified according to whether they are delivered and controlled by the same department, provided by a third party or transacted on behalf of the state. Full implementation of the reform program will take several years because of the need for extensive personnel training and institutional retooling. Efforts to refine and expand the output budgeting system will concentrate on (i) establishing management and budget plans for all on-budget agencies early in the fiscal year; (ii) reducing the number of outputs and simplifying the associated cost structure; and (iii) developing rolling three-year estimates of specific outputs for long-term planning. The public sector reform program, along with stable financial policies, should contribute increasingly to private capital formation.

Improving Private Sector Development. The Government recognizes the centrality of the private sector as the engine of economic growth, and it is increasingly forging a development partnership between public and private sectors in pursuing private sector development. Given the relatively low share of private investment in the past and the need to progressively improve the role of the private sector for accelerating economic growth, the Government has intensified its efforts in this area. In early 1996, the Government clarified and articulated its approach towards the private sector and economic development through a "Statement of Economic Strategy: A New Partnership." In particular, progress has been made recently on reducing and streamlining import tariffs, privatization of public enterprises, and on the adoption of APEC non-binding conditions.

Privatization. The principal feature of the Government's private sector development strategy is the privatization of state-owned enterprises in order to raise efficiency and productivity while reducing the size and presence of government in the economy. Considerable progress has been made in formulating a privatization strategy and in improving the poor performance of State owned enterprises. The Government needs to focus its efforts on divestitures slated for 1996/97 and to take other measures as necessary to improve the performance of state enterprises.

Addressing Financial Sector Liberalization. The existing system of direct instruments creates distortions in the financial market. Plans for moving to a system of indirect controls have been in place for some time and considerable progress has been made in establishing the preconditions for a successful transition, particularly with respect to a stable macroeconomic environment and consolidating the fiscal position. While the process needs to be carefully managed, efforts could now be intensified to carry out the transition during the course of 1998.

Other Reforms. Land reforms, agricultural diversification, rationalization of industrial incentives, and streamlining of investment procedures are required if Samoa is to become more competitive.

Government Policies and Objectives

For several years now, the Government has declared its commitment to promoting the private sector as the engine of economic growth. To this end, it has withdrawn from some activities altogether; important public services have been contracted out to private businesses; state-owned enterprises have been wholly or partially privatized; deep cuts have been made to public expenditure; and a forceful start has been made to reforming the fiscal system. The Government is also committed to forging an effective partnership with the private sector and other stakeholders. In that regard, the Government intends to work towards the creation of a "level playing field" on which businesses can compete on equal terms with one another, with foreign competitors and with the public sector in its role as a supplier of goods and services. Measures to promote growth in the private sector will center on the creation of a less regulated economic environment; continuing reform of the fiscal system, which will increasingly incorporate incentives to investment without the need for discretionary intervention; the sale of shares in state-owned enterprises (primarily to citizens); and determined efforts to make and more available for productive use.In May 1998, the Government announced in the 1998/99 budget a comprehensive package of fiscal reforms focusing particularly in the areas of tariff and taxation reform. These reforms, which include major reductions to import duties and excises, and further cuts to income tax, are intended to complete the taxation reform process begun five years ago.

SOLOMON ISLANDS

Population:	**386,700 (1996)**
GDP:	**US$363 million (1996)**
GNP Per Capita:	**US$960 (1996)**

Introduction

With a GNP per capita of US$960 in 1996, the Solomon Islands economy is dominated by export-oriented production involving tree crop plantations, commercial fishing and logging; a large public services sector; and a subsistence agricultural sector that provides the main source of livelihood for a vast majority of the population. Foreign aid inflows have, until recently, averaged about 20 percent of GDP annually; nonetheless, improvement in social and economic conditions has been slow.

Recent Economic Developments

The economy of Solomon Islands is experiencing an unprecedented financial crisis characterized by mounting domestic and external debt service arrears, falling revenues and high expenditures, and an over-exposed financial sector that threatens the economic and financial stability of the country. The problem is compounded by an unsustainable rate of deforestation, falling social indicators, deteriorating physical infrastructure, and a bloated public sector. In recent months, a collapse in the prices of log exports amidst accumulation of unsold inventories (since late 1997) has brought felling to a standstill.

Fueled by intensive exploitation of forest resources, in part due to soaring international timber prices, real GDP growth averaged more than 6 percent per year during 1992-95, considerably higher than rates achieved in earlier years. This has, however, masked deep underlying weaknesses in the financial system and delayed the onset of a severe crisis. Real GDP slowed considerably to an estimated 3.5 percent in 1996, down from a high growth of over 7 percent in 1995. The slowdown in the economy in 1996 is in part attributable to a weak agricultural sector caused by adverse weather, depressed fish catch and output of key agricultural commodities, mainly copra, coconut oil, palm oil and cocoa. A moderate improvement in log shipments in 1996 in response to favorable prices was insufficient to offset the unfavorable developments in the other agricultural sub-sectors. The real GDP is estimated to have declined by about 1 percent in 1997.

After declining from over 14 percent (annual average percentage change) in early 1996, to 7 percent in early 1997, consumer inflation (Honiara Retail Price Index) has edged higher over 1997 reaching nearly 9 percent by mid-year. Inflationary pressures remained higher than the country's trading partners through the rest of 1997, resulting in continued downward pressure on the exchange rate or further losses in competitiveness. The Solomon Islands dollar was devalued by 20 percent in December 1997, reversing the earlier appreciation of the real effective exchange rate.

Increased logging revenues combined with expenditure restraint, shrank the fiscal deficit to about 2.4 percent of GDP in 1995 from the equivalent of over 13 percent of GDP in 1991. However, continued government borrowing from the domestic banking system resulted in a significant accumulation of external and domestic arrears as legal limits of such borrowing were reached. The fiscal deficit has increased further since 1995 as a result of a sharp downturn in revenue reflecting a decline in commodity prices and more subdued domestic demand conditions after the completion of a number of major construction projects. With budget control and reporting completely lacking, overly optimistic projections diluting transparency and continuing difficulties in raising offshore and domestic funds, a substantial further build-up in arrears has occured. By end-December 1997, total government outstanding arrears amounted to an estimated SI$192 million.

The external reserve position improved in 1996, having deteriorated steadily during 1992-95. This development mainly reflects improvements in the current account due to higher log export receipts and high net capital inflows from official as well as private sources. Foreign exchange reserves increased to SI$110 million at end-1996, up sharply from SI$52 million at end-1995. However, by end-December 1997, gross official reserves had dwindled to SI$98 million (equivalent to about 2.6 months of import cover), as the financial crisis deepened.

SOLOMON ISLANDS: KEY MACRO INDICATORS, 1992-96

	1992	1993	1994	1995	1996
Indicator Levels (US$ million)					
GDP (at current prices)	209.0	260.2	295.5	327.2	362.6
Govt. Revenues	105.6	107.4	139.1	128.3	148.6
Govt. Expenditures	120.7	127.7	155.3	145.8	168.4
Govt. Budget Deficit (-)	-15.1	-20.3	-16.3	-17.5	-19.8
Exports (fob)	102.9	129.1	143.7	168.3	162.4
Imports (cif)	111.5	136.9	142.2	154.5	151.5
Current Account Balance (after grants)	-8.1	-7.4	-2.2	9.3	4.9
Gross Reserves	22	19	17	15	32
Macro Balances (% GDP)					
Budget Deficit (-)	-7.2	-7.9	-6.6	-2.4	-4.0
External Current Account Balance	-3.9	-2.8	-0.7	2.8	1.4
Foreign Public Debt	44.1	35.9	33.0	30.7	27.3
Domestic Public Debt (Central Govt.)	31.3	30.5	32.0	30.8	27.2
Memo Items (% p.a.)					
GDP growth	9.5	2.0	5.2	7.0	3.5
Consumer Inflation (%)	10.7	9.2	13.3	9.6	11.8
Terms of Trade (% change)	3.1	49.4	9.6	-13.2	7.8
Reserves (mo. imports, fob)	2.3	1.7	1.4	1.2	2.6

Source: Data provided by Solomon Islands authorities; IMF Staff Reports, 03/98; Staff estimates.

Key Development Issues

Improving Financial Management.
Financial mismanagement resulting in large fiscal deficits and high debt levels, has been the main cause of substantial macro-economic imbalance and financial instability in recent years, particularly since 1995. Despite substantial growth in government revenue between 1991-96, averaging around 18 percent per annum, similar growth rates in public expenditure resulted in fiscal deficits amounting to around SI$340 million in total over these years. The vast majority of government expenditure over this period was on recurrent spending, while around 95 percent of the deficit has been financed from the domestic banking system and the National Provident Fund, and, in more recent times, through the build-up of arrears. Debt service costs have increased by around 15 percent per annum over these years. Addressing the high fiscal imbalances is the key to promoting a more sustainable pattern of social and economic development.

Improving Forest Management. Since 1992, developments in the forestry sector have been driven by a rapid increase in the rate of exploitation–log exports increased 85 percent to about 550,000 cu. meters. Since then, timber exports have increased at over 10 percent in volume terms each year and are estimated to have been about 811,000 cu. meters in 1996. The level of cut associated with these export levels is unsustainable relative to Solomon Islands endowment of forest resources. A 1993 forest inventory placed the sustainable level of cut at about 300,000 cu. meters per year. Thus, the rate of logging during the past five years has been double what sustainable practice would warrant and it is estimated that at these rates of harvesting, the Solomon Islands will deplete its forest resources within 10 to 15 years. Clearly, urgent action is required to drastically reduce the present unsustainable rate of timber harvesting. Measures to be considered include halting new logging licenses as well as phasing out export tax exemptions. The Government's initiative to cancel all remissions and exemptions effective November 10, 1997, is laudable and should be built upon by reviewing all other exemptions granted by the Foreign Investment Board over the medium term. The already weak export price monitoring system for log exports has collapsed following imposition of austerity measures earlier in 1997. Re-establishment of a working price monotoring system should be a priority as it would significantly strengthen revenue collection from the forestry sector.

Civil Service Reform and the Wage Bill.
After years of rapid growth in public employment, the Government is confronted with a severe financial crisis and is hard pressed to even pay its employees, let alone provide resources for goods and services. In line with the rise in the number of civil servants, the wage bill has claimed on average about 40 percent of total recurrent budgetary resources over the past three years and has crippled government finances to the extent that service delivery has stagnated in many areas and deteriorated in some, such as maintenance of physical infrastructure particularly in rural areas. To address the present financial difficulties, it is imperative that the wage bill is brought under control in the short run through a reduction in allowances and abolishing vacant positions. Over the medium term, the Government would need to implement a well-designed civil service reform program based on the following priciples: (i) a clear definition of the core functions of government—namely provision of basic services, ensuring national security and maintaining law and order; (ii) identification and removal of duplicate functions and privatization of those areas where the private sector could be an efficient agent;

(iii) corporatization of certain functions to improve accountability, enhance productivity and rationalize staffing and operations; and (iv) reduction of numbers through removal of over-aged and unauthorized employees. The Government's stated policy intention to reduce the number of government ministries from 16 to 10 needs to be pursued in the context of a comprehensive civil service reform program.

Public Enterprise Reform. Public enterprises and statutory authorities number over 30 in the Solomon Islands and contribute significantly to GDP. However, despite significant capital investment over past decades, overall returns to the Government have been negligible and services are generally poor. Statutory Authorities, which number over 20, have constituted a substantial drain on public finances. The Government needs to formulate a strategy to reduce its role in many of these areas, improve service delivery and increase cost recovery. Priorities should be the Ports Authority, Electricity Authority, Commodity Export Marketing Authority and the Livestock Development Authority. In the case of enterprises, there is a clear need for evaluation and restructuring. The performance of the Investment Corporation of Solomon Islands has been poor with no dividends being paid to the Government in 1997. All enterprises in the corporation's portfolio need to be evaluated and business plans established for loss-making ones including privatization options.

Government Objectives and Policies.

The Government is intending to undertake a Policy and Structural Reform Program aimed at addressing the present financial difficulties while restructuring the economy to achieve sustainable and broad-based economic growth. The required structure and decisionmaking committes have been established to build consensus and support amongst various stakeholders, including Parliament, Government Caucus, Cabinet, the public sector, the private sector, trade unions, civil society, and the donor community. The organizational structure, as well as a broad reform agenda focusing on macro and micro economic policies to achieve stability and enhance productivity and competitiveness, including public sector reform to reduce the Government's involvement in economic activities and promote private sector–led growth, has been developed and presented in a government document entitled, "Framework of Policy and Structural Reform Programme."

TONGA

Population:	**106,000 (1996)**
GDP:	**US$178 million (1996)**
GNP Per Capita:	**US$1,640 (1996)**

Introduction

With a per capita income of US$1,640 in 1996, the Kingdom of Tonga ranks among the lower middle income group of developing nations. The economy is dominated by agriculture and services. Agriculture accounts for 37 percent of GDP and consists mainly of production of domestic food crops and a narrow range of cash crops (copra, squash, vanilla, and melons). Services account for nearly 50 percent of GDP, of which about one third is government activity in one form or another.

Tonga has achieved commendable social progress as reflected by a life expectancy of 69 years (1995) and a literacy rate of almost 100 percent (in the Tongan language), among the highest in the region. Tonga's favorable physical environment, and rich cultural traditions, including the extended family systems, land ownership, and the role of the churches, have endowed the population with a safe and secure lifestyle. However, further improvements in the quality of life may not be possible without sustainable economic growth and corresponding increases in government revenues. Budget constraints may force cuts in expenditures. Eventually, social progress made to date may suffer erosion unless adequate resources are maintained through sustainable economic growth.

Recent Economic Developments

After years of expansion in the early 1990s when economic growth was largely fueled by booming squash exports, real GDP growth slowed considerably in 1994/95 and turned negative in the subsequent year. The sluggish performance of economic activity in recent years is largely attributable to poor performance of the squash industry which has been adversely affected in recent times by diseases, marketing problems, soil depletion, shortage of crop financing and growing foreign competition. From 4,000 metric tons in 1989/90, squash production and exports, which had risen to 18,000 metric tons by 1993/94, dropped sharply to 9,000 tons in 1995/96. The 1995/96 crop was also adversely affected by a severe drought as well as quota restrictions. The export quota, which had been unpopular with growers, was abolished in advance of the 1996/97 planting season. Nonetheless, affected by diseases, the 1996/97 harvest was only about 10,000 tons, while prices were about half the 1995/96 level.

Reflecting movements in squash exports, Tonga's traditionally large trade deficit began to widen in 1993/94 as squash exports declined, while imports, fueled by expansionary financial policies, continued to rise. Consequently, the external current account balance swung into substantial deficit by the mid-1990s compared to surpluses achieved during the early 1990s. The current account deficit averaged nearly 6 percent of GDP during 1993/94 to 1994/95 and improved a bit in 1995/96 as imports declined. Gross external reserves fell sharply to 4.8 months of import cover by end-1995/96 compared to a level of 8 months in 1992/93. This sharp decline largely reflects a massive expansion of domestic credit to the private sector by as much as 38 percent in 1994/95, with the entry of two new commercial banks. However, credit expansion had moderated to 10 percent in 1995/96 following tighter monetary policy.

After recovering from a period of large deficits during the late 1980s and early 1990s, fiscal policy again turned expansionary in 1993/94. The recurrent surplus, which had reached 4 percent of GDP in 1993/94, declined to 2.5 percent of GDP in 1995/96, stemming largely from a 10 percent cost of living adjustment to government wages in 1995/96. The overall fiscal balance swung from a surplus of nearly 3 percent of GDP in 1993/94 to a deficit of 1 percent of GDP in 1995/96. Contributing to the deficit was also an expansion in development expenditures brought on by large aid-financed projects in infrastructure, particularly power development and road upgrading. The 1996/97 budget restrained recurrent expenditures to the 1995/96 level but envisaged a further increase in development expenditures. The deficit is estimated at about 6 percent of GDP.

TONGA: KEY MACRO INDICATORS, 1991/92 to 1995/96

	1991/92	1992/93	1993/94	1994/95	1995/96
Indicator Levels (US$ million)					
GDP (at current prices)	140.1	145.0	151.9	164.8	177.9
Govt. Revenues	53.6	61.5	65.4	75.9	75.2
Govt. Expenditures	62.7	58.5	58.2	77.0	77.0
Govt. Budget Deficit (-)	-9.1	2.9	7.2	-1.1	-1.8
Exports (fob)	16.6	11.9	16.1	14.0	13.6
Imports (fob)	48.0	50.8	54.5	69.8	62.0
Current Account Balance (after grants)	3.8	3.0	-8.0	-9.8	-4.7
Gross Reserves	29.6	35.6	31.5	25.7	25.0
Macro Balances (% GDP)					
Budget Deficit (-)	-6.6	1.8	2.8	-3.2	-1.0
External Current Account Balance	2.7	2.1	-5.3	-5.9	-2.6
Foreign Public Debt	36.3	35.9	34.0	38.1	33.6
Domestic Public Debt (Central Govt.)	10.1	12.5	7.4	7.1	6.6
Memo Items (% p.a.)					
GDP growth	0.3	3.8	5.9	2.3	-0.4
Consumer Inflation (%)	8.7	3.1	2.4	0.3	2.8
Terms of Trade (% change)					
Reserves (mo. imports, fob)	7.4	8.4	6.9	4.4	4.8

Source: IMF Staff Reports, 01/97; Data provided by Tongan authorities.

Consumer inflation has been trending downwards in recent years compared to the early 1990s when inflation soared to around 10 percent as a result of the expansionary fiscal stance, large wage increases, high import prices and a drought. Following fiscal restraint, inflation declined to under 1 percent in 1994/95 despite the acceleration in credit, the impact of which was mainly felt in the external sector. Inflationary pressures are estimated to have picked up moderately during 1995/96.

Government Objectives

The declared objective of the budget for FY95/96 was to build on three pillars: (i) keeping public spending levels in line with available resources, implying restraint in the wages bill in particular; (ii) reduction of the role of the Government in commercial activities; and (iii) a focus on improving the efficiency of the public sector rather than increasing the already heavy tax burden, falling essentially on external trade and a narrow domestic tax base. Similarly, the overriding objective in the FY96/97 budget is to control public spending by limiting recurrent outlays, including the rationalization of the civil service and maintenance of an open and competitive economy. The Government intends to revise the tax structure to make it more equitable, simple, efficient and market-oriented.

Key Development Issues

Restoring Economic Growth. With the recent downturn in the economy and growing unemployment, particularly among the youth, there is an urgent need for the Government to pursue a higher growth development strategy based on a progressive right-sizing of the public sector and a gradually increasing role for the private sector. A key issue is the ability of the private sector to generate adequate jobs for a growing labor force, as well as exports to offset potential declines in aid and remittances. Export growth in particular requires high priority, and calls for concerted efforts in agricultural diversification, fisheries, tourism development, and encouragement of other manufactured exports. Such a strategy is attainable since Tonga does not suffer from major macroeconomic imbalances.

Public Sector Reform and Privatization. With a public service of 4,195 employees in FY 95/96, the size of the wage bill amounted to an estimated 54 percent of total current expenditures. As a result, nonwage expenditures have suffered, given the limits of the resource envelope. Specifically, the allocation for operations and maintenance has contracted to an estimated 7 percent of the total, with adverse consequences for asset maintenance. Likewise, funds available for the purchase of goods and services has also contracted. Also, at the aggregate level, the existence of a large number of public enterprises places a heavy burden on public finances. In this regard, the Government should consider, as a first step, privatizing commercial activities of relatively low strategic value that would be efficiently managed by the private sector. Thus, a need exists for a progressive right-sizing of the public sector, with public expenditures and public enterprises focused on core areas and leaving other activities to the private sector, church groups and nongovernment organizations. Plans to privatize public enterprises and/or commercialize provision of public service need to be revitalized to enable the Government to concentrate better on its priority areas where it has comparative advantage. Churches and NGOs should be encouraged to carry on and further develop their service provision roles in the social and other sectors, since it would be more cost effective for the Government to provide additional support to these organizations rather than duplicate their efforts.

Improving Effectiveness of Public Expenditure. Fiscal constraints and the changing role of the state imply a need to reconsider inter-sector investment priorities and intra-sector priorities to improve the development effectiveness of public spending. There is considerable scope for improving the development effectiveness of intra-sectoral priorities. Education should be refocused to better meet the skill demands in the economy. Also, rather than spending government funds on expanding physical facilities, and thus duplicating the efforts of non-government organizations, such funds could be better spent on improving the quality of education by the development of curricula and teaching materials, supply of text books and teacher training. In health, greater priority needs to be given to preventive vis-à-vis costly curative care. This calls for more expenditures on cleaner water supply, public health programs, health education and public awareness campaigns. In agriculture, allocations for research and extension services could be increased progressively through savings elsewhere in the sector. In infrastructure, greater focus needs to be given to rehabilitation and operations and maintenance while new investment requires more careful scrutinizing to ensure that priority is given to projects which maximize social benefits.

VANUATU

Population:	**173,000 (1996)**
GDP:	**US$252 million (1996)**
GNP Per Capita:	**US$1,290 (1996)**

Introduction

The economy of Vanuatu is dualistic with about 80 percent of the population engaged in subsistence or small scale agriculture, primarily copra, cocoa, and beef production. The formal economy is dominated by services, including government, tourism and an offshore financial center. Vanuatu faces a variety of geographical constraints to economic development including vulnerability to external shocks, remoteness from major markets and large distances from constituent islands. While poverty is limited, development has been focused on urban centers—particularly Port Vila—resulting in increasing regional income inequality and growing rural-urban migration. Vanuatu has strong economic potential in agriculture, forestry and tourism. External aid has been generous by international standards, yet growth has been slow and uneven.

Recent Economic Developments

Vanuatu has maintained macroeconomic stability throughout the 1990s with an annual inflation rate averaging 3 to 4 percent, gross international reserves equivalent to 7 to 8 months of imports, and a low debt service ratio. However, real per capita income has stagnated despite generous amounts of foreign assistance, and the disparity in living standards between the formal and subsistence sectors remains wide.

The economy grew at 3.2 percent in 1995 and by a further estimated 3 percent in 1996, reflecting increased earnings from agriculture, especially copra and cocoa, receipts from tourism and growth in construction activities. Copra, the main agricultural product, continued to expand as trees recovered from the cyclones of 1992 while cocoa production recovered from a severe drought in 1994. Construction output in 1995 was strengthened by the construction of several public investment projects including the Law School of the University of the South Pacific and the hydro-dam project in Luganville.

Consumer inflation, on an annual average basis, slowed from 2.7 percent in 1994 to 1.7 percent in 1995, broadly in line with Vanuatu's major trading partners. Despite the introduction of a new turnover tax, the decline in inflation in 1995 was largely attributable to a significant reduction in import tariffs and a sharp decrease in rents as new dwelling units increased in response to a housing loan scheme introduced by the National Provident Fund. Inflationary pressures remained low in 1996.

The external position has remained favorable in recent years, as higher international copra prices boosted export earnings while tourism receipts grew steadily. The current account deficit narrowed from nearly 6 percent of GDP in 1994 to 4 percent in 1995 and remained low in 1996. Gross external reserves have averaged about seven months of import cover since 1994, marginally down from an import cover of eight months attained at end-1993.

The overall fiscal deficit narrowed to under 2 percent of GDP in 1995, down from 3 percent of GDP in 1994, due in part to lower development expenditures. However, with increased development outlays relating to some airport upgrading activities, the deficit is estimated to have widened in 1996 to a little over 2 percent of GDP. Given the emphasis on tourism as a potential high-growth sector, airport upgrading has become a strong development expenditure priority in recent years.

VANUATU: KEY MACRO INDICATORS, 1992-96

	1992	1993	1994	1995	1996
Indicator Levels (US$ million)					
GDP (at current prices)	190.0	195.6	214.4	238.3	252.4
Govt. Revenues	71.8	66.4	79.7	89.3	94.4
Govt. Expenditures	78.2	69.0	86.2	93.1	99.8
Govt. Budget Deficit (-)	-6.4	-2.6	-6.5	-3.8	-5.4
Exports (fob)	23.6	22.7	25.0	28.3	30.2
Imports (fob)	68.3	65.8	74.6	80.0	86.4
Current Account Balance (after grants)	-4.3	-6.2	-12.1	-9.8	-11.5
Gross Reserves	41.8	45.7	43.6	48.3	51.3
Macro Balances (% GDP)					
Budget Deficit (-)	-3.4	-1.3	-3.0	-1.6	-2.1
External Current Account Balance	-2.3	-3.2	-5.6	-4.1	-4.6
Foreign Public Debt	21.3	21.7	21.7	20.2	18.7
Memo Items (% p.a.)					
GDP growth	-0.7	4.4	2.6	3.2	3.0
Gross Investment/GDP (%)	28.6	27.8	28.8	31.0	..
Consumer Inflation (%)	4.1	1.7	2.7	1.7	2.5
Terms of Trade (% change)	22.2	-15.1	36.5	12.7	-0.8
Reserves (mo. imports, fob)	7.3	8.3	7.0	7.2	7.1

Source: IMF Staff Reports, 05/96.

Government Objectives

In view of the developmental challenges facing the country, the Government, in collaboration with the Asian Development Bank, has recently formulated a Comprehensive Reform Program (CRP) aimed at attaining sustainable economic growth, improving public sector management and ensuring good governance. At a recent Consultative Group Meeting held in Noumea late July 1997, the Government expressed strong commitment to implementing the reforms articulated under the CRP, with wide participation from civil society.

Key Development Issues

Strengthening Public Finances. Although macroeconomic events remain favorable, fiscal control was weak under previous administrations. Determined efforts are needed to bring the recurrent budget into balance through strict control over the wage bill and the supplementary appropriation process, while strengthening the revenue effort through tax reforms as foreign grants are likely to decline over the medium term. The new Government has improved budgetary control and a strong fiscal position is expected within two years.

Improving Economic Growth. In view of the stagnation of per capita incomes, economic growth needs to be enhanced. Structural reforms, private sector development, and fiscal consolidation are essential to improving the growth prospects of the economy over the medium term. Concerted efforts are needed to promote private sector development, and economic diversification including improvements in the efficiency of the public sector, and physical and social infrastructure. Diversification in the agricultural sector, new investment in industry and growth in tourism and other service sectors is much-needed to broaden the economic base and reduce vulnerability to change in the external environment, as well as improve the growth prospects of the economy. The Government needs to sustain implementation efforts under the CRP in order to address, *inter alia*, structural impediments to growth.

BUDGETING IN THE PACIFIC MEMBER COUNTRIES— FROM CASH MANAGEMENT TO OUTPUT MANAGEMENT

A central theme of this Regional Economic Report is the dominant role of government in most sectors of the member economies. However state-led growth has not fulfilled aspirations for growth in incomes per head. There is a clear need to improve the development effectiveness of public expenditure.

A particular cause for concern in many member countries is the domination of government spending by recurrent outlays. This has been at the expense of public investment in growth-promoting infrastructure and other 'development-friendly' expenditures.

A large component of budget outlays in the PMCs reflects long-standing programs which may not directly address the current development priorities of the member governments. The combination of large government spending and low spending on development-related activities is likely to be a significant cause of the slow pace of development in the region.[1] Achieving a reduction in total government spending while simultaneously increasing the development-promoting component of that spending is likely to be an important step towards realizing current development aspirations.

However, the successful achievement of this twin budget objective poses a daunting challenge for budgeting processes, even for developed countries with sophisticated budgeting systems. The dilemma of how to downsize government while simultaneously increasing development expenditures can be resolved in various ways: by privatization, corporatization, and outsourcing. A further solution is the improvement in budgeting processes. This Annex addresses some of the options available to PMCs attempting to reallocate public sector resources to development-reinforcing activities while simultaneously reducing the overall size of government.

CENTRAL CONTROL VERSUS ALLOCATIVE FLEXIBILITY

Traditional approaches to budget management are characterized by separate appropriations of funds for what is sometimes a bewildering variety of line items. These cover agency running costs (split into numerous components ranging from postage expenses to wages) and program costs (split by program and activity within program). This line item–intensive approach to budgeting is intended to increase the transparency of the uses made of funds by program departments, and to strengthen central

---

[1] A 'development-friendly' budget therefore typically:

- contributes to reducing the overall share of government in economic activity, lowering the financial burden government places on private enterprise, while at the same time

- increases government investment on infrastructure, education, health and other high priority areas which will assist the development process.

agency control of each component of their spending. Detailed line item budgeting also reduces the likelihood of under-spending or over-spending of appropriations by enabling central agencies to monitor how much is spent in each area or activity.

Developing countries, including the PMCs, have typically adopted a traditional, line item–intensive approach to budgeting. This approach is particularly relevant to the budgeting task in developing countries since it provides maximum control by central agencies over spending which in many cases is undertaken by program agencies with relatively undeveloped financial management skills and systems. Scope for inconsistent decisionmaking and corrupt behavior is minimized, while central control over the total level of spending is maximized.

However, traditional systems of budgeting which emphasize strong central control over the fine detail of program agency spending can also build inflexibility into budget processes. Such budgeting systems may reduce the responsiveness of program agencies to changing budget priorities by restricting their ability to redirect funding from existing line items to new activities. The price paid for strong control of spending from the center is likely to be weaker incentives for program agencies to fund new spending priorities by reducing spending on line items already in the budget. The following section discusses some possible reasons for this.

TRADITIONAL BUDGETING AND LINE AGENCY COMPETENCIES

A side effect of traditional, line item–intensive budgeting is that spending agencies have a reduced need to develop the in-house financial and policy analysis skills required to allocate resources between their various divisions and activities. Highly prescriptive budgets inhibit agency capacity to identify options for redirecting spending between its various activities—which line items are cost-effective and which are not, or where new spending needs

might be funded by reduced funding of other activities (funding reallocations) rather than additional funding from the budget. Internal prioritizing decisions are pre-empted by the existence of multiple line items which prescribe in detail how the program agency is to spend the envelope of funds made available to it.[2]

The role of line agencies tends towards that of an agency for dispensing funds rather than planning for their optimal use.

Highly centralized budget processes are also likely to reduce line agency capacity to implement such internal reallocations. Significant financial and resource management skills are often required at the agency level in order to re-assign resources internally. Activities already in the budget, such as the wages of permanent public sector employees, are difficult to avoid, and staff reallocation encounters geographical, organizational and human resource management barriers. However, the development of broader resource management skills is inhibited when the primary role of spending agencies is to dispense funds in predetermined ways rather than to manage broader envelopes of resources in a flexible manner.

The result is likely to be something of a bias in highly centralized budget processes towards the preservation of activities which already have a place in the budget, at the expense of those which do not. From the perspective of a program agency with a limited internal skill base, reducing the scale of programs already in the budget (for which line items are established) may be a much harder option to handle than postponement of outlays not already in the budget (and to which resources have not yet been committed).

---

2 A qualification is where scope exists for transfer of resources by virement approved by the Finance Ministry.

When requested to reduce their total spending, for example, program agencies with poorly developed financial and management skills may find it easier to delay new capital projects or postpone repairs and maintenance not yet provided for in the budget than to propose resource transfers from existing line items for which tenured staff, often with narrow skills, would have to be re-deployed to other areas of the agency.

Reflecting this, traditional line item–intensive budgeting has some drawbacks in circumstances where faster development will require reductions in total movement spending combined with increased outlays on development promoting infrastructure and maintenance. The strength of traditional budgeting, with its strong emphasis on central control, lies in the delivery of established patterns of government spending rather than managing reallocations within those patterns in response to the newly emerging development priorities. The complex nature of the policy goal for PMC governments (lower aggregate spending combined with increased spending on development-reinforcing activities) may therefore be best served by more flexible budget processes than those relying on strong central control via large numbers of line items.

Re-tuning of budget processes to the challenges of more rapid development is therefore a potentially important step towards breaking from the region's 'big government/low development' malaise.

FIJI'S EXPERIENCE

In Fiji, as in the other PMCs, the share of public investment in GDP is low. The evidence suggests that this is in part associated with institutional shortcomings in program agencies. Even in Fiji, where reform of budget processes has proceeded furthest among the PMCs, there remain major deficiencies in the financial and policy analysis skills of program agencies. As in the other PMCs, the tendency for budgets involving large numbers of centrally approved line items has tended to reduce the incentive for program agencies to develop internal capacity to analyze priorities and internally re-direct resources in response to changing budget objectives.

This weakness in financial and policy analysis skills of program agencies has several effects. One is lack of technical capability on the part of such agencies to implement development projects in any number. Program agencies are reluctant to propose more investment projects for consideration in the annual budget process than they feel they have the capacity to manage. This hesitancy occurs because of global public sector staff ceilings applying in Fiji and each agency's first and foremost need to cover the wage costs of existing programs.

In addition, many of the new spending proposals prepared by program agencies in the course of the Fijian budget process are regarded by the central agencies as not being 'bankable' due to shortcomings in the standard of policy analysis and project justification. This reflects the existence of many unfilled positions in the planning units of key departments and lack of skills and experience of existing staff.

Restricted capacity for reallocating resources within spending agencies, combined with the ceiling on total spending implied by Fiji's target of a balanced budget by the year 2000, results in a tendency for the postponement of new infrastructure investment and other 'development-friendly' activities in favor of continued high levels of recurrent spending on activities with an established place in the budget. Overall deficit reduction objectives and resource management inflexibility at the agency level combine to edge out new infrastructure and related spending, and the budget system becomes an impediment to the increase in development sought by the Government.[3]

A central challenge for budgeting systems in the PMCs is, therefore, to reallocate funds within agencies from historically inherited programs to development reinforcing activities. This entails a transition from programs with high and generally unavoidable wage costs to programs in which infrastructure and maintenance spending provides a better environment for development. In the past, this has been postponed when the agency budget is under pressure from the center.

THE CONTENTS OF THIS ANNEX

Budget processes capable of achieving greater internal flexibility in spending and a capacity for re-prioritization between appropriations are not currently a feature of budgeting in the PMCs. Capacity for internal allocative flexibility needs to be strengthened; it is important that management freedoms regarding the disposition of budget funds be devolved from Finance Ministries to spending agencies in order to permit them to undertake more flexible, goal-focused management.

However, it is equally important for devolution of managerial freedoms to avoid running ahead of the internal financial management and policy capabilities of spending agencies in the member countries. A precondition of devolution is that, from the outset program agencies should be able to re-prioritize and reallocate the broader pools of resources available to them in a competent manner if the waste of resources is to be avoided.

Unfortunately, this leads to a sequencing problem. Devolving of responsibility for managing funds to program agencies should not

---

[3] Alternatively, if government spending does expand in support of growth and social goals, this may be at the expense of overall deficit management and the public sector grows in total size (budget augmentation is substituted for budget reprioritization.)

run ahead of financial and policy competence in those agencies. However, the development of capacity to re-prioritize and reallocate resources within line agencies is unlikely to develop in isolation from devolution to them of more responsibility for making internal resource allocation decisions.

The dilemma for the PMCs is how to strike a balance between maintaining centralized budget control in order to curb the growth of 'big government' on the one hand, and providing a catalyst (in the form of increased line agency discretion in the use of resources) for development of the financial and policy skills needed for budget flexibility on the other. The capacity to increase spending in those areas supporting development while simultaneously reducing the bottom line deficit is a benchmark of a budget process which is 'development-friendly.'

The central focus of this Annex is on two budgeting tools which may help resolve this dilemma in the PMCs. These tools are a medium-term framework for the budget, and devolution of management freedoms to program agencies. Taken together, these two budgeting tools can contribute to the growth of financial and policy autonomy in program agencies while minimizing counterproductive loss of control from the center.

These budget tools are part of the public sector reform packages in a number of countries. Among the PMCs, Fiji has grappled most vigorously with the problem of combining allocative flexibility with overall budget control. A far-reaching public sector reform program was initiated some years ago and momentum is currently high. This Annex, therefore, takes Fiji as a case study in the use of the two tools.

BUDGET TOOL 1. A MEDIUM-TERM BUDGET FRAMEWORK

Budgeting in a medium-term framework has a variety of meanings. However, a common element is the extension of the estimates of outlays for each line item in the annual budget for an additional year or more. These out-year estimates are normally rolled forward by one year with each new annual budget. The first out-year figures then become the baseline for next year's budget without being subjected to as full a review process as is associated with a budgeting system which is restricted to a one-year time frame.

In some systems (for example the Australian) the first out-year figures flow automatically into the next year's budget without further revision (except for technical adjustment for inflation etc.). In other systems of forward estimates–based budgeting, such as that of Fiji, the forward estimates for the coming budget year are reviewed in the early stage of the budget process as a matter of course. That review focuses particularly on whether capital projects are proceeding as planned and whether some deferral or acceleration in spending on the forward estimates figure is desirable for specific projects.

In the case of Fiji, the budget has been prepared in a three-year rolling forward estimates–framework for an extended period of time. Budget estimates for ongoing capital projects and operating costs are based on the sum already contained in the forward estimates, adjusted for technical factors and reviewed for appropriateness.[4] Forward estimates of operating costs are also reviewed by the Ministry of Finance. Early in the budget process, a paper goes to the Budget and Aid Coordinating Committee seeking approval of the

updates of the forward estimates.[5] This then becomes the baseline budget. Added to this is a new policy not already included in the forward estimates. New policy costings are negotiated between the line agency and the Ministry of Finance for both budget year and out-years, with the out-year figures being added to the forward estimates.

Forward estimates–based budgeting can help to rectify the imbalance between recurrent and capital spending which characterizes the PMCs, as well as the tendency to provide insufficient funds for the operation and maintenance of completed projects. It may contribute in a number of ways.

First, it is easier for new development-promoting expenditures to find a place in a three-year budget cycle than in a single-year cycle because the availability of funds is less of a constraint on budget planning for the out-years of a three-year cycle. The multi-year budget cycle establishes a time frame (the period of the rolling forward estimates) and a formal budgeting framework (the forward estimates themselves) within which program agencies have to identify the reallocations from existing budget items required to fund new development-promoting expenditures written into the forward estimates. It provides a formal framework within which program agencies can plan the re-prioritization of budget outlays.

Second, a medium-term budgeting framework allows additional lead time between incorporating a project in the budget cycle and project commencement. This provides line agencies with time for detailed project appraisal and project design work, rather than the ad hoc justification for new spending proposals frequently resorted to by agencies due to the

---

[4] Capital projects which are already underway are re-prioritized by the Ministry of Planning and Ministry of Finance (in conjunction with the implementing agency) on the basis of operational reports on the state of progress on the project. Projects which have been ongoing for three years are subject to more formal review, in which the current achievement is compared with the original proposal.

[5] The Budget and Aid Coordinating Committee is chaired by the Permanent Seeretary of Finance and includes the Permanent Secretaries of the Public Service Commission, National Planning and (on aid issues) Foreign Affairs.

pressures of an annual budget process. The result is likely to be an improvement in the quality of investment proposals put forward by program agencies.

Third, a medium-term budgeting framework also lightens the work load in the actual budget process, contributing to a better quality process. This is because the out-year components of the capital budget can be examined after the current budget year component has been completed, allowing better screening of projects being considered for inclusion in the forward estimates.

Fourth, a medium-term budgeting framework can assist the integration of aid-funded projects with the overall allocation of budget resources. Better coordination of donor priorities with the overall development strategy and opportunities for growth is sought by the Fiji Government.

Fifth, an important benefit from the use of a medium-term budgeting framework relates to future spending on operations and maintenance. In the case where each budget is treated as a separate annual 'event' the implications of current decisions to fund development projects for future spending on operations and maintenance can be overlooked. However, in a medium-term budgeting framework, these future spending commitments should be included in the forward estimates when the project itself is introduced to the budget.

Sixth, budgeting within a multi-year term framework rather than on a year by year basis encourages the Government to prepare medium-term targets for the overall level of budget spending and deficit. This imposes a discipline on annual budgeting and a consistency check on each annual budget against the Government's medium-term fiscal objectives.

However, perhaps the main advantage of the use of a forward estimate–based budget cycle is that it provides a framework for integrating the medium-term development plan with the annual cash budget. The dominance of the annual budget (with its large share of recurrent spending) over the development plan is likely to be a factor contributing to the Pacific region's dilemma of 'over-size government' combined with deficient development expenditures. Adoption of a multi-year framework for budgeting propels the budget process beyond the annual ritual in which development expenditures are determined as a residual after meeting existing program commitments historically embedded in successive annual budgets.

Why should this be so? The medium-term budgeting framework encourages a strategic focus on resources which can be mobilized from within spending agencies themselves, whereas in a purely annual budget context, the focus tends to be on the funds which can be obtained from outside the agency.

The three-year time frame for the budget cycle therefore allows the reallocation of funds between existing and new activities to be formally structured into the budget decision making process itself. This increases the likelihood of agencies responding to the government's medium-term development priorities by redirection of resources within the overall targets for public spending. Over the medium-term budgeting cycle, existing program commitments can become variables rather than constraints. The longer cycle, therefore, affords a formal framework for downsizing total spending while increasing spending on development-friendly activities.

FIJI'S EXPERIENCE

The Fijian Government's multi-year budget strategy provides an example of the scope for reallocating resources towards development priorities within a medium-term budgeting framework. The Fijian Government has announced an objective of restoring the budget deficit to balance by the year 2000. To this end it has imposed a ceiling on new public sector employment and a target reduction of 5,000 persons by 1999. This constrains bids for additional resourcing by line agencies.

To achieve a balanced budget by 2000 line agencies other than those responsible for infrastructure, education, health and agriculture (the four core contributors to the development strategy) are to receive virtually no funds for new policy. Moreover they are required to pay a 1.5 percent efficiency dividend in the budgets for 1997, 1998 and 1999. A later cabinet decision requires an additional 1 percent to be paid in 1998, 2 per cent in 1999 and 3 per cent in 2000. The four core agencies, on the other hand, have been given increases in funding in the forward estimates which are linked to GDP.

This medium-term budget strategy effectively forces the new development-focused spending by the core ministries to be funded by reallocations from the non-core ministries over the next three years. As a result, the commitment to a balanced budget by the year 2000 is reconciled with increased spending on development-friendly activities. A further element of reallocation within non-core ministries themselves is achieved by the requirement that their annual efficiency dividend be at the expense of line items for operating costs rather than capital items in those agencies.[6]

---

[6] A shortcoming of the arrangement is that there is no pressure on the core ministries themselves to divert funds from the less cost-effective activities that exist in their own portfolio. In this regard, the identification of core ministries is a blunter weapon for reallocating budget resources than a similar budgeting approach based on the identification of core activities rather than ministries.

It is also worth noting that the integration of development plan and annual budget is not complete in Fiji, since there is not currently a medium-term rolling set of capital expenditure estimates incorporating new investment projects. Such estimates were prepared in 1994 for the key sectors of infrastructure, health and education and updated in 1995. However they have been discontinued due to the claims made on technical personnel by the annual budget.

BUDGET TOOL 2. DEVOLUTION OF MANAGEMENT FREEDOMS FROM CENTRAL TO PROGRAM AGENCIES

The first budgeting reform discussed above—establishment of a medium-term budgeting framework—helps make decisions to re-prioritize the use of existing resources, a more common feature of the budget decisionmaking process. The second area of budget reform, which is discussed in the present section, involves devolution of greater management freedoms to program agencies than under the current, highly centralized, budgeting arrangements of the PMCs.

What is meant by decentralized budgeting? Rather than central agencies prescribing in great detail the uses to which running costs and program costs are to be put by program agencies (by bringing down budgets composed of large numbers of highly detailed line items), greater freedom is given to program agencies themselves to allocate funds between their various activities. Line items are 'broad banded' and agencies are authorized to apportion funds within the bands according to the most cost-effective means they can identify for meeting the Government's priorities.

This has two major advantages. First, it allows those with the detailed knowledge of how programs are operating to shift administrative and program funds between spending categories in pursuit of best value for money. Moreover, waste associated with end of year 'spend-ups' in each of the former, narrower, appropriation is minimized. Additional resources can be swung behind activities encountering problems or delays or for which the Government indicates a high priority.

The second advantage is that line agencies will need to develop their ability to make internal resource allocation decisions not required under traditional line item intensive budgeting. In response to the need to prioritize their own use of resources, they will be under pressure to develop the technical capacity for internal budgeting and policy analysis. A central resource-coordinating function is likely to emerge in the program agency for this purpose. Monitoring of the resources used by internal divisions of the agency, together with the results generated by each division's activity, becomes routine for this group in the course of deciding how broader envelopes of resources allocated to the agency are to be distributed between its constituent parts.

Within-agency performance monitoring is likely to apply both to the use made of funding for running costs (which in the extreme case are received by the agency as single appropriation) as well as program appropriations. Such information is normally not generated under traditional, line item–intensive budgeting. Even if it were to be available within the line agency, it is unlikely to be made available to central finance ministries in the course of developing the detailed spending splits under traditional budgeting processes.

Once program agencies have developed an ability to identify their less cost-effective activities, it is easier for governments to make the decision to fund new development activities by cutting existing spending rather than by increasing budget outlays. The necessary spending cuts can be allocated within each spending agency to those of its activities, the contraction of which causes least damage to the Government's other political and social objectives.

THE 'CHICKEN AND THE EGG'

A prerequisite of greater financial management freedoms for line agencies is the following. It is vitally important for spending agencies to have developed in the early stages of the budget reform process a core of financial and management skills sufficient to ensure that their increased managerial prerogative leads to more cost-effective budget outcomes, rather than bureaucratic empire building or corrupt

practices. A line department which is granted greater freedom of financial management, but in which the senior executive has failed to develop internal resource allocation skills, may suffer from inefficient splits of broad-banded appropriations between its various activities. Where resource management is weak, the distribution of funding between its constituent divisions may reflect the internal politics of the agency, or the perpetuation of historic shares, rather than the cost-effectiveness of their various claims on funding.

In this circumstance, the devolution of financial freedoms may reinforce (rather than modify) the existing tendency for over-large outlays on personnel and wages and under-spending on the capital and O&M side of the budget (which is able to be postponed).

The depth of financial and policy management skills in PMC program agencies is clearly limited at the present stage of development in the region. For example, in Fiji each of the core ministries now has its own planning unit. However, ability to fill positions in the planning units with experienced policy analysts is limited, and lack of policy analysis skills seem to be a constraint on the development of new policy proposals, even in core agencies such as the Department of Health.

This presents a 'chicken and egg' problem. Financial and policy analysis skills are likely to develop at the line agency level only in response to a more devolved decision making environment and a need to make significant resource allocation decisions within the agency. However, central coordinating agencies are reluctant to devolve resource management freedoms until those skills are already in place in line agencies.

The Fijian budget reforms throw some light on how this circularity might be resolved. Increased performance consciousness on the part of program agencies, together with the deepening of their financial and policy analysis skills, is a central element of the budget reforms in Fiji.

However, a Management Effectiveness Review in 1994 suggested that the management of program agencies was unclear about the goals it was pursuing in its day-to-day activities.

Several steps have been taken to address this problem. From 1998, each permanent secretary is to have a performance agreement and five-year contract, together with greater freedom to make decisions about the use of resources in his or her agency. This includes delegation of power by the Public Service Commission from 1998 to allow agency heads to appoint staff up to middle management level.[7]

One important complementary reform has been the introduction of corporate planning in each agency. This provides a link between the national priorities for government spending and the internal prioritization of resource use by each program agency.

A further closely related development is the introduction of performance contracts for middle management. It is intended that the performance agreements should clearly reflect the Government's priorities as reflected in the agency's corporate plans and government policy documents.

Performance contracts are a highly effective device for ensuring that the day-to-day activities of middle management reflect to the maximum possible extent the current priorities of the Government. They also allow retrospective assessment (in the course of periodic review sessions with supervisors) of how far the individual manager has been effective in translating the Government's current priorities through his or her achievements during the course of the working year.

---

[7] Creation of new positions will remain the prerogative of the Public Service Commission. However, a second stage of the reform is to devolve this function when performance is established for the first stage.

A further important development in this context is the training of senior public sector executives in management skills appropriate to their new, more devolved, operating environment. In Fiji, the Public Service Commission is working to develop senior executive training in program agencies. The Ministry of Planning is also addressing this problem by working closely with spending agencies and seconding staff to agencies in need of capacity building.

A significant step towards recognizing the role of Fijian line agencies in managing outputs as well as inputs was taken in the 1997 budget papers. These papers included a set of activity descriptions alongside budget items for the first time. These descriptions are input or workload orientated rather than output or outcome orientated. However, they are an important first step towards the more transparent acceptance of responsibility on the part of line agencies for the deliverables associated with each of their budget appropriations. Inputs are no longer to be made available to an agency without reference to the outputs and outcomes expected in return. This focuses spending agencies on why money is being given to them to spend (and on what it is to be spent). It is intended that the 1998 activity descriptions will have an increased emphasis on output targets. This is an initial step in upgrading departmental information systems beyond cash management to output management.

A parallel development relates to the enhancement of the national audit office function in Fiji. This involves the extension of audit activities beyond cash flows to include output/outcome effects of line agency spending. While cash flows are audited against the appropriations defining the uses for which the cash is made available, performance auditing involves assessing the results of the spending against the reasons for making the funds available. This move from cash to performance auditing is a logical counterpart to the emerging responsibility of line agencies for output management as well as cash management.

Finally, as a long-term goal, an accrual accounting framework is to be introduced in Fiji to enable the full resource cost of activities to be identified by the spending agencies. This is currently being piloted in four departments.[8]

WILL PROGRAM AGENCIES RE-PRIORITIZE THEIR SPENDING?

Public sector budgeting in the PMCs is characterized by short planning horizons and limited capacity to re-prioritize spending in pursuit of current development objectives. These defects are in part attributable to lack of resource and policy management skills in program agencies—skills which are slow to develop where spending splits are dictated in great detail by central agencies. However, tight central control of spending is unlikely to be relinquished until the skill base in program agencies itself improves.

This Annex has discussed two budgeting tools—multi-period budgeting and decentralized financial management—which might help to cut through this dilemma. Once the capacity of program agencies to re-prioritize their activities has improved, a solution to the broader challenge of reducing the size of movement while increasing spending on development-related activities is within reach.

Political will is still required to force line agencies to fund new activities (or extensions to existing activities) by internally reprioritizing spending, rather than adopting the 'soft option' of a request for additional funding from the budget. Recent Fijian experience emphasizes the importance of commitment at the political level in order to make reprioritization an effective alternative to budget augmentation. If line agencies are able to appeal directly to the Cabinet for exemption from the requirement for internal reallocation, the advantages of the system in ensuring budget discipline will rapidly erode. A case in point is the Fijian Commodity Development Framework, for which spending was approved in 1997 outside the normal budget process for what was then a non-priority department, and which is likely to make the achievement of the target of a balanced budget by the year 2000 difficult.

Cross fertilization of budgeting skills from finance to program ministries has a particularly important role to play in increasing technical capacity in the latter. However, there is a further sequencing problem here. In many member countries the scope for central agency fertilization of financial and policy skills in the program agencies is limited by shortages of the same skills in the central agencies themselves. Even in Fiji, where budget reform has proceeded furthest, there are multiple vacancies in the Ministry of Planning, and that agency is itself in need of a capacity-building program to match its vigorous promotion of development.[9] In some of the smaller PMCs, the first priority is to reinforce the generic budgeting skills of the Finance Ministries themselves.

---

[8] A further issue in Fiji is that shortage of financial and policy analysis skills is exacerbated by the large number of ministries and agencies (in excess of fifty) which means that scarce policy analysis and development skills are very thinly spread. Some rationalization of administrative structures into larger units, better able to support viable policy analysis and development capability, may be an important precondition for spending agencies developing the skill base necessary for their role in re-prioritizing spending.

[9] Budgeting reform such as that underway in Fiji also requires excellent coordination between the central coordinating departments themselves. Cooperation between the Public Service Commission and the Ministry of Finance has improved since 1994 in response to the zero staff growth policy introduced then, and the need to coordinate this with the new spending authorized in the budget. The Ministries of Finance and Planning also work together closely, although there may be scope for improved cooperation in vetting investment proposals emerging from program agencies.

External pressure for reform of budget processes in circumstances where central agencies themselves have not yet established the depth of modern budgeting skills is as likely to slow the development process as to speed it up. It is essential for finance officers to understand the purpose of budget process reforms being made in their country if their role in transfer of financial and policy management skills to spending agencies is to be effective. In some member countries, the first stage of reform should be the boosting of the skills of the central agencies themselves.

In this regard there may be a substantial leverage effect from the funding and organization of regional budget workshops for officials from central coordinating agencies.[10] Such training should preferably focus on middle level finance officials, particularly desk officers with ongoing contact with spending agencies. However, senior staff would need to be involved to ensure that the content of such courses is closely linked to the particular reforms envisaged by the central coordinating agencies. It is likely that assistance by international agencies in building human resource skills in the central coordinating ministries will have a substantial leverage effect on skill acquisition in the public sector as a whole.

---

[10] An example is the course in budgeting practice piloted by the Economic Development Institute of the World Bank in Singapore in September 1997.

THE STRUCTURE AND SIZE OF THE PUBLIC SECTOR IN THE PMCS

A1   THE STRUCTURE OF THE PUBLIC SECTOR

Despite their small size, the PMCs have adopted reasonably complex government structures, with most operating at least two levels of government. Fiji, the Solomon Islands, the Marshall Islands and Kiribati operate national and local governments. The local government system, which is mainly concerned with the provision of basic services such as waste disposal and local roads, can be extensive. For example, in Fiji, there are two city councils, nine town councils, 12 rural local authorities and 14 provincial councils. In FSM and the Solomon Islands, state governments operate as well as national and local level governments. Traditional government systems can also play an important role, being perhaps strongest in Samoa and Tonga where only one level of formal government operates (see Table A3.1).

The PMCs are noted for the large number of government agencies they support. For example, in Fiji the organizational structure presents 18 ministries and another 57 departments or agencies (see Table A3.2). A total of 31 separate budget-supported agencies are identified in the Fiji budget, while there are 21 in one of the smaller PMCs, Kiribati (see Table A3.1). The large number of agencies is characterized by the duplication of basic administrative functions, the fragmentation of the skill base and coordination problems because of the compartmentalization of functions.

The ministries/departments are broadly similar across the PMCs. As illustrated by the list of Fijian, Tongan and Samoan agencies presented in Tables A3.2 and A3.3, there are normally separate agriculture, forestry and fishing departments and an industry agency focused on processing activities. The health, education and defense portfolios tend to account for around a third of civil servants. The infrastructure-based agencies of transport and public works also tend to be large employers. One reason for the large number of agencies in the PMCs is that the various administrative tasks of government (e.g. auditing, revenue collection) tend to be split into separate ministries or departments.

Table A3.1: Organizational Characteristics of PMC Governments

	Fiji	Solomon Islands	Vanuatu	Samoa	FSM	Tonga	Marshall Islands	Kiribati
Levels of government	2	3	2	1	3	1	2	2
Number of separate budget-supported agencies	31	25	n.a.	28	n.a.	28	n.a.	21
Number of public enterprises [a]	30	7	13	21	32	20	11	26

n.a.   not available.
a   That is, enterprises either 100 percent or majority government-owned.
Sources: PMC authorities.

Most PMCs support a generous number of public enterprises. The highest number of enterprises occurs in FSM, a result of duplication by the four state governments (e.g. of the utilities). There are 32 enterprises recorded in FSM and 30 in Fiji, with the Solomon Islands, Vanuatu and the Marshall Islands supporting the lowest number of public enterprises (see Table A3.1). The size and composition of the public enterprise sector in the PMCs is referred to below.

Table A3.2: The Ministries and Departments of Fiji

Ministry/Department		Ministry/Department	
1	Office of the Prime Minister	8	Ministry of Information, Women and Culture
	Office of the President		Information, Technology and Computing Services
	Cabinet Office		Services
	Public Service Commission		Women and Culture
	Elections Office		Fiji Museum
	Ombudsman's Office		National Archives
	Parliament of Fiji (Legislature)		Fiji Arts Council
	District Administration	9	Ministry of Labor and Industrial Relations
	Multi-Ethnic Affairs		Arbitration Tribunal
2	Ministry of Education and Technology	10	Ministry of National Planning
3	Attorney General		Bureau of Statistics
	Law Reform Commission	11	Ministry of Youth, Employment Opportunities
	Central Liquor Board		and Sports
	Cinematography Censorship Board	12	Ministry of Local Government and Environment
	Hotel Licensing Board		Environment
4	Ministry of Finance		Town and Country Planning
	Treasury		Local Government
	Customs and Excise		Housing
	Government Supplies	13	Ministry of Health
	Information, Technology and Computing	14	Ministry of Commerce, Industry, Cooperatives
	Services		and Public Enterprises
	Inland Revenue		Cooperatives
	Printing and Stationery		Fair Trading
5	Ministry of Justice and Home Affairs	15	Ministry of Lands and Mineral Resources
	Judicial		Lands and Survey
	Public Prosecutions		Mineral Resources
	Fiji Prison Service	16	Ministry of Agriculture, Fisheries and Forests
	Social Welfare		Agricultural Tribunal
	Stamp Duties		Forestry
	Administrator General	17	Ministry of Communication, Works and Energy
	Titles Office		Public Works
	Registrar General		Energy
	Immigration Department		Regulatory Unit
	Fiji Military Forces		Marine
	Fiji Police Force	18	Ministry of Transport and Tourism
6	Ministry of Foreign Affairs and External Trade		Road Transport
	External Trade		Tourism
7	Ministry of Fijian Affairs and Agricultural		Civil Aviation
	Lands and Tenants Act (ALTA)		Meteorological Services
	ALTA		
	Native Lands Commission		

Source: Fiji Public Service Commission.

Table A3.3: The Ministries and Departments of Tonga and Samoa

Tongan Ministry	Samoan Department/Ministry
Agriculture	Agriculture
Audit	Attorney General
Central Planning	Audit
Civil Aviation	Broadcasting
Crown Law	Customs
Customs	Education
Education	Foreign Affairs
Finance	Health
Fisheries	Internal Affairs
Foreign Affairs	Inland Revenue
Government Store	Justice
Governor, Ha'apai	Legislative
Governor, Vava'u	Labor Department
Health	Lands and Environment
Inland Revenue	Lands and Title
Justice	Ministry of Transport
Labor, Commerce and Industry	Ministry of Youth, Sports and
Lands	Culture
Marine and Ports	Prime Minister's Office
Palace Office	Post Office
Police	Police and Prison
Post Office	Public Service Commission
Prime Minister's Office	Public Works
Printing	Statistics
Prison	Trade Commerce and Industry
Sales tax	Treasury
Statistics	Women's Affairs
Tonga Visitor's Bureau	
Treasury	
Public Works	

Sources: Tonga Office of Establishments, Samoa Department of Finance.

A2 THE SIZE OF THE GENERAL GOVERNMENT SECTOR

For the purposes of assessing the size of the public sector, this Annex distinguishes between the general government sector and the public enterprise sector. General government is defined to include national, state and local governments and those statutory authorities without a commercial focus.

The most commonly used measure of the size of government is the ratio of total government expenditure to GDP. The 1997 World Development Report focused on comparisons of the level of government consumption on the basis that it helps clarify the critical division of output between the public and private sectors. Reliable data on government consumption in the PMCs are limited, and instead comparisons are presented of current expenditure. Further insights are also provided by comparing the level of general government employment and the wage and salary bill.

Table A3.4 presents measures of the size of the general government sector based on the ratio of government expenditure to GDP. In broad terms, the greater the sophistication of the PMC economy, the smaller the relative size of government. Hence, Fiji, Vanuatu, the Solomon Islands and Samoa have the smallest general government sectors. The heavily aid-dependent countries with poorly developed private sectors —the Marshall Islands, Kiribati and FSM—are shown as having markedly larger general government sectors. Over the past five years, these more heavily governed PMCs have made some progress in reducing the size of general government. However, their ratio of government expenditure to GDP is still very high.

The most recent estimates of total general government expenditure to GDP range from 34 to 87 percent. The ratio of current expenditure to GDP is estimated to be in the range of 28 to 63 percent, with the wages and salaries bill of general government accounting between 11 to 29 percent of GDP.

Chart A3.1 shows the split of expenditure in Fiji's general government sector among the three components—the national government, local government and the noncommercial statutory bodies. The national government is shown to dominate expenditure, a feature of all PMCs except for the FSM. In the FSM, the State Governments are the main service providers and collectively are much larger than the National Government.

Table A3.4: Expenditure on general government in the PMCs

General government expenditure as a share of GDP (percent)

	Fiji [a]	Solomon Islands [b]	Vanuatu [b]	Samoa [a]	FSM [a]	Tonga [a]	Marshall Islands [b]	Kiribati [b]
Most recent estimate								
- total expenditure	34	45	39	57	78	51	87	87
- current expenditure	28	29	26	31	62	28	59	63
- wages and salaries	13	11	12	11	29	15	22	26
Average over the previous five years								
- total expenditure	33	53	39	67	82	50	99	99
- current expenditure	29	33	27	36	65	28	73	60
- wages and salaries	14	13	12	12	29	15	23	24

a   The most recent estimate is for the year 1996, with the average being for the period 1992 to 1996.
b   The most recent estimate is for the year 1995, with the average being for the period 1991 to 1995. 1995 estimates are used when the latest available GDP figure is for 1995.
Sources: PMC authorities, IMF Recent Economic Developments.

An implication of high ratios of government expenditure to GDP is the small size of the private sector in the PMCs. This is a result of a range of factors controlled by the PMCs, such as crowding out by the public sector, but it also arises because of factors outside their control. These factors include natural impediments to cost of transport. When looking at ratios of expenditure to GDP, the conclusion that government is big could have more to do with the small size of the private sector than a genuinely excessive government.

Alternative measures of the size of government are presented in Table A5 based on the level of general government employment. Within the group of PMCs, FSM still stands out as being very heavily governed. It is estimated that for every 1,000 residents (of all ages), 90 are employed in general government. The Governments of the Marshall Islands and Kiribati are not as dominant as is suggested by the ratios of expenditure to GDP. The employment measure suggests Tonga is one of the more heavily governend PMCs, while the Solomon Islands is shown as probably having the smallest general government sector. Never-

theless, even in the Solomon Islands, it is etimated that one in four formal employees is a civil servant.

Chart A3.1: General government expenditure on wages and salaries in Fiji

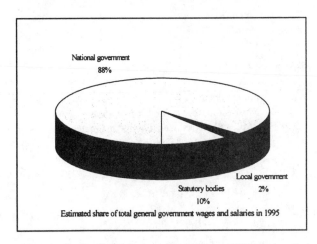

Estimated share of total general government wages and salaries in 1995

Sources: Preliminary data supplied by the Fiji Bureau of Statistics.

Because of a lack of data, international comparisons of the size of government must rely on the ratio of central government expenditure to GDP. In the body of this report, comparisons are presented of the size of government in 62 low and middle income countries. Government expenditure in the PMCs stood out as being unusually high, with the PMCs providing the three highest ratios of expenditure to GDP. The picture was even more startling when the level of government wages and salaries as a share of GDP was considered. While these international comparisons should be seen as indicative only because of the many measurement problems, they clearly point to the presence of large governments in the PMCs.

It may be argued that this conclusion is the result of comparing the PMCs with much larger countries. Larger countries may realize economies in government as they may be able to spread a 'fixed cost' of establishing government over a wide range of activities. In contrast, in countries with small populations the fixed cost of government may lead to relatively large governments.

However, this is not evident from the data. The Cook Islands, with a population of only 20,000, has a lower ratio of central government expenditure to GDP than four of the PMCs. Comparisons with the Caribbean countries are also revealing. The Caribbean countries share with the PMCs small populations and a broadly similar structure of government (although average incomes are higher in the Caribbean). Ratios of expenditure to GDP for the PMCs and the Caribbean countries are shown in Charts A2 to A4. The size of government is fairly steady across the Caribbean countries and the less extreme PMCs. This suggests that a small population does not necessarily demand a relatively large government.

The comparisons with the Caribbean countries also lend support to the conclusion that governments in the PMCs tend to be large

Table A3.5: Employment by general government in the PMCs

	General government employment (most recent estimate) [a]							
	Fiji	Solomon Islands	Vanuatu	Samoa	FSM	Tonga	Marshall Islands	Kiribati
Best estimate of persons employed	31,943	9,585	5,286	6,409	9,413	5,203	2,189	3,574
Employment per 1,000 residents	40	25	31	39	90	53	39	46
Share of labor force (percent)	11	n.a.	n.a.	n.a.	36	n.a.	n.a.	n.a.
Share of formal workforce (percent)	29	29	n.a.	27	n.a.	40	25	51

n.a.   not available.
a   Most estimates are for 1995 or 1996.
Sources: PMC authorities, Consultants' estimates.

Chart A3.2: Central government expenditure in the PMCs and the Caribbean [a]

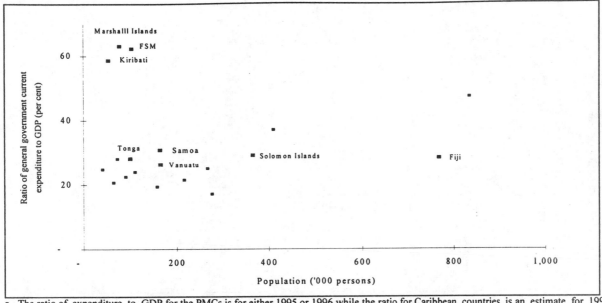

a   The ratio of expenditure to GDP for the PMCs is for either 1995 or 1996 while the ratio for Caribbean countries is an estimate for 1994. The Caribbean countries included are Antigua, Bahamas, Barbados, Belize, Dominica, Grenada, Guyana, St . Kitts -Nevis, St. Lucia, St. Vincent and Suriname. The population estimates are for either 1994 or 1995. Expenditure in the FSM includes state government expenditure.
Sources: PMC authorities, IMF Recent Economic Developments, World Bank 1997a, World Bank 1996a, AusAID 1997.

Chart A3.3:   Central government current expenditure in the PMCs and the Caribbean [a]

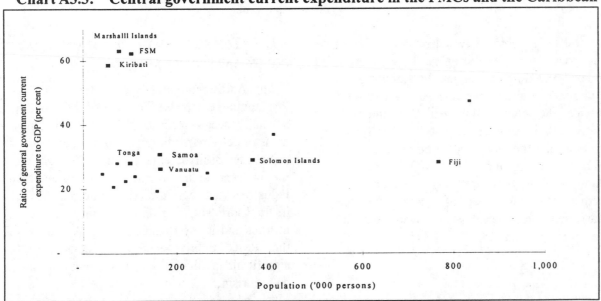

a   The ratio of current expenditure to GDP for the PMCs is for either 1995 or 1996 while the ratio for Caribbean countries is an estimate for 1994. The Caribbean countries included are Antigua, Bahamas, Barbados, Belize, Dominica, Grenada, Guyana, St. Kitts-Nevis, St. Lucia, St. Vincent and Suriname. The population estimates are for either 1994 or 1995. Expenditure in the FSM includes state government expenditure.
Sources: PMC authorities, IMF Recent Economic Developments, World Bank 1997a, World Bank 1996a, AusAID 1997.

Chart A3.4: Central government expenditure on wages and salaries in the PMCs and the Caribbean a

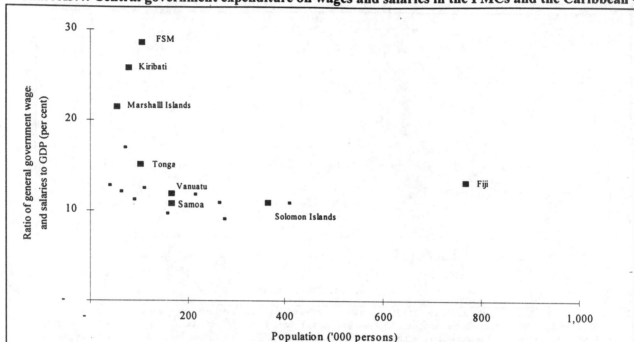

a The ratio of wage and salary expenditure to GDP for the PMCs is for either 1995 or 1996 while the ratio for Caribbean countries is for either 1994 or 1993, except for Trinidad and Tobago which is for 1992. The Caribbean countries included are Antigua, Bahamas, Barbados, Belize, Dominica, Grenada, St. Kitts-Nevis, St. Lucia, St. Vincent and Suriname. The population estimates are for either 1994 or 1995. Expenditure in the FSM includes state government expenditure.
Sources: PMC authorities, IMF Recent Economic developments, World Bank 1997a, World Bank 1996a, AusAID 1997.

A useful insight into what is driving the size of PMC governments can be gained by comparing the level of aid per capita and the amount spent on civil servants for each resident. Chart A3.5 presents the comparison, which suggests a positive relationship between the availability of aid funds and the money spent on civil servants (with Fiji being the only PMC where this relationship is not evident). Hence the internationally high level of aid to the PMCs clearly tends to finance large governments by international standards.

A3   *THE SIZE AND COMPOSITION OF THE PUBLIC ENTERPRISE SECTOR*

Table A3.6 summarizes the involvement of PMC public enterprises in areas of the economy normally seen as contestable. That is, those areas of activity readily open to competition and private sector involvement. The table highlights the widespread involvement in resource-based industries (e.g. agriculture, fishing, electricity), in transport (shipping and air transport), in the utilities and in the finance sector. A number of the PMC public enterprises also have a significant involvement in manufacturing, trade and tourism.

Chart A3.5: Aid and the expenditure on wages and salaries in the PMCs [a]

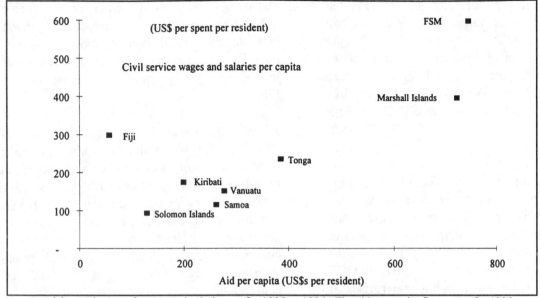

a   Most estimates of wages and salaries are for 1995 or 1996. The aid per capita figures are for 1995.
Sources: Data supplied by PMC authorities, Consultants' estimates, AusAID 1997.

Table A3.6: Readily contestable activities of public enterprises [a]

Activity	Fiji	Solomon Islands	Vanuatu	Samoa	FSM	Tonga	Marshall Islands	Kiribati
Resource-based industries								
Livestock/dairy	■	■	■	■			■	
Sugar	■							
Other agriculture	■	■		■	■	■	■	■
Fishing	■	■	■	■	■	■		■
Forestry	■		■	■		■		
Quarrying				■		■		
Manufacturing and trade								
Food products				■		■		■
Government supplies and printing	■	■						
Retail/wholesale				■	■	■	■	■
Utilities								
Electricity	■			■	■	■	■	■
Telecommunications		■	■	■	■	■	■	■
Broadcasting	■		■	■	■	■	■	■
Transport								
Shipping	■	■				■	■	■
Air transport	■	■	■	■	■	■	■	■
Finance								
Commercial banking [b]	■		■	■	■		■	■
Other finance	■		■	■				■
Tourism								
Hotels	■			■		■		■
Tour activities			■					

a   That is, activities engaged by government-controlled enterprises that could be readily undertaken by the private sector.
b   Other than the provision of a Development Bank.

Fiji has the best data on the operation of its public enterprises. Preliminary public sector accounts available for 1990-95 provide an estimate of value-added for financial and nonfinancial public enterprises. In 1990, the value-added of nonfinancial enterprises amounted to 12 percent of GDP, but it had risen to 24 percent by 1995. Financial enterprises contributed a further 3 percent of GDP in both years.

International comparisons of the public enterprise sector are made difficult by a shortage of data and potential differences in the way the sector is measured (e.g. in defining what constitutes a public enterprise). Indicative comparisons with other developing countries are presented in Chart A3.6. The share of GDP accounted for by Fiji's public enterprises is significantly higher than the average or other middle income economies, Asia and the Latin American and Caribbean region. It is closer to that seen in countries of a lower income, such as in Sub-Saharan Africa. While such comparisons need to be treated with caution because of potential weaknesses with the data, they do point to a relatively large public enterprise sector in Fiji.

An estimate is also shown of the share of GDP accounted for by public enterprises in FSM. FSM public enterprises are shown as accounting for a fairly typical share of GDP. However, it is important to realize that aid is very high in FSM and injects a considerable amount of income via government. Hence, a very large general government sector leads to a small public enterprise sector when ratios to GDP are considered.

Chart A3.6: The importance of nonfinancial public enterprises [a]

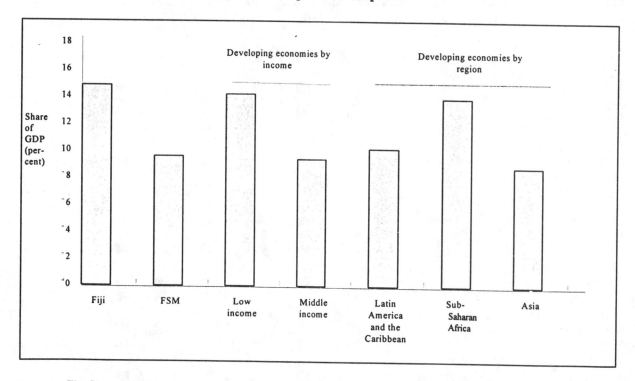

a   The figure for Fiji is an average for 1990-95 while the figure for FSM is an average for 1994-95. The group averages are estimates of the unweighted average for 1986-91. The definitions used in preparing the data may vary between countries and thus the data may not be directly comparable.
Sources: Preliminary data from the Fiji Bureau of Statistics, World Bank 1995, EMAPT 1997.

The size of the FSM public enterprise is made clearer in Table A3.7. The table summarizes public enterprise employment in the PMCs, and suggests that the Fijian and FSM public enterprise sectors are similar in size. By these employment measures, the public enterprise sector in Samoa, Tonga and Kiribati is relatively larger than Fiji. Comparisons of employment with other developing countries point to large public enterprise sectors by international standards (see Table A3.8)

Table A3.7: Employment by public enterprises in selected PMCs

	Public enterprise employment (most recent estimate)				
	Fiji	Samoa	FSM	Tonga	Kiribati
Best estimate of persons employed	12,198	2,893	1,479	1,702	1,824
Employment per 1,000 residents	15	18	14	17	23
Share of workforce (percent)	4	n.a.	6	n.a.	n.a.
Share of paid workforce (percent)	11	12	n.a.	13	26

Sources: PMC Authorities

Table A3.8: International comparisons of public enterprise employment

Selected PMCs	Share of paid workforce (percent) [a]	Other developing countries	Share of paid workforce (percent) [b]
Fiji	11	Low-income economies	16
Samoa	12	Middle-income economies	6
Tonga	13	Latin America and the Caribbean	2
Kiribati [c]	26	Africa	22
		Asia	3

a   The data for the PMCs are the most recent estimate, usually 1994 or later.
b   The group averages are estimates of the unweighted average for 1986-91. The definitions used in preparing the data may vary between countries and thus the data may not be directly comparable with the PMC data.
c   Includes employment in financial enterprises.
Sources: Unpublished data from the Fiji Bureau of Statistics, World Bank 1995.

Tables A3.9 to A3.16 provide a detailed list of public enterprises in the PMCs. Data on employment are also provided where available.

Table A3.9: Public enterprises in Fiji

Enterprise	Employees in 1994 (persons)
Fully government-owned	
Post Fiji Ltd.	1,385
Telecom Fiji Ltd.	n.a.
National Trading Corporation Ltd. [b]	11
Rewa Rice Ltd.	44
Unit Trust of Fiji (Management) Ltd.	2
Yaqara Pastoral Company Ltd.	35
Viti Corps Company Ltd.	n.a.
Partially government- owned	
Majority shareholding	
Air Pacific Ltd.	601
Fiji International Telecommunication Ltd.	101
Fiji Pine Ltd.	780
Fiji Sugar Corporation Ltd.	3,100
Pacific Fishing Company Ltd.	1,000
Minority shareholding	
Air Fiji Ltd.	134
Fiji Reinsurance Company Ltd.	9
Pacific Forum Line Ltd. [c]	64
Shipbuilding (Fiji) Ltd.	n.a.
Commercial statutory bodies	
Civil Aviation Authority of Fiji	771
Fiji Broadcasting Commission	140
Fiji Electricity Authority	1,200
Fiji Meat Industry Board	73
Housing Authority [d]	240
National Bank of Fiji Asset Management Bank [e]	616
National Bank of Fiji	n.a.
Ports Authority of Fiji [f]	221
Public Rental Board	n.a.
Other commercially orientated government agencies	
Drainage and Irrigation Department	32
Government Handicraft Center	5
Government Printing and Stationary Department	135
Government Supplies Department	226
Marine Fleet Section	517
Public Works Department	963
Forestry Department—Hardwood Plantations	n.a.
Public Trustee	n.a.
Meteorological Service	n.a.
Sub-total [g]	12,198

Readings to Table A3.9
n.a. not available
a In 1994, 1,385 persons were employed in Fiji Posts and Telecommunications Ltd., which was subsequently separated into Post Fiji Ltd. and Telecom Fiji Ltd.
b A holding company for five agricultural-based companies.
c Shipping charter company.
d A provider of housing finance.
e The manager of the assets of the collapsed Bank of Fiji.
f Ports management, stevedoring and cargo handling.
g Excluding enterprises for which employment numbers are unavailable and companies with a minority government shareholding.
Source: Fiji authorities.

Table A3.10: Public enterprises in the Solomon Islands

Enterprise
Fully government-owned [a]
Solomon Island Printers Ltd.
Solomon Islands National Shipping Services Ltd.
Sasape Marina Ltd.
Solomon Airlines Ltd.
Partially government-owned
Majority-owned
Solomon Taiyo Ltd. [b]
Solomon Telekom Co. Ltd.
Development Bank of Solomon Islands
Minority owned
Solomon Islands Plantation Ltd.
Kolombangara Forestry and Plantation Ltd.
Air Pacific Ltd.
Pacific Forum Line Ltd.

a This list excludes known commercially oriented departments such as post, civil aviation and government supplies.
b Classified as part of the agriculture and fishing sector.
Source: Solomon Islands authorities.

Table A3.11: Public enterprises in Vanuatu

Enterprise

Fully government-owned
    Development Bank of Vanuatu
    Port Vila Fisheries Ltd.
    South Pacific Fishing Company Ltd.
    Air Vanuatu (Operations) Ltd.
    Vanuatu Internal Air Services (Vanair) Ltd.
    National Bank of Vanuatu
    Vanuatu Holdings Ltd.

Partially government-owned
Majority-owned
    Vanuatu Abattoirs Ltd.
    Metenesfl Estates Ltd.
    Tour Vanuatu Ltd.

Minority-owned
    Telecom Vanuatu Ltd.
    Bel-Mol Cattle
    Ifira Wharf and Stevedoring Ltd.
    Ifira General Services Ltd.
    Union Electrique Du Vanuatu Ltd.

Statutory corporations
    National Housing Corporation
    Vanuatu National Provident Fund
    Vanuatu Broadcasting and Television Corporation

Source: Vanuatu authorities.

Reading to Table A3.12
n.a.   not available
a A provider of housing finance.
b A cargo shipping vessel.
c Superannuation fund and provider of business and home loans.
d The holding company of the airline, Polynesian Ltd.
e Involved in the sale/lease of former West Samoa Trust Estates Corporation land.
f Involved in ports management, stevedoring and cargo handling.
g Activities include quarrying, the production of concrete blocks and dredging.
h Activities include cattle and copra production.
i Involved in general maintenance and engineering.
j A producer of processed meat products.

Table A3.12: Public enterprises in Samoa

Enterprise	Employees in 1996 (persons)
Fully government-owned	
Accident Compensation Board	16
Airport Authority	202
Agriculture Stores Corporation	67
Development Bank of Western Samoa	124
Electric Power Corporation	469
Housing Corporation [a]	14
MV Forum Samoa [b]	26
National Provident Fund [c]	123
Polynesian Airlines (Holding) Ltd. [d]	0
Polynesian Ltd.	355
Samoa Land Corporation [e]	15
Samoa Shipping Services [f]	124
Special Projects Development Corporation [g]	80
Televise Samoa Propriety Ltd.	21
Western Samoa Water Authority	166
Western Samoa Life Assurance Corporation	45
Western Samoa Shipping Corporation	105
Western Samoa Trust Estates Corporation [h]	229
Partially government-owned	
Majority-owned	
Western Samoa Breweries	132
Minority-owned	
Air Pacific	n.a.
BOC-Samoa/ Samoa Industrial Gases	16
Brugger Industries Ltd. [i]	12
Computer Services Ltd.	26
Hellaby's Samoa Ltd. [j]	24
National Pacific Insurance	14
Pacific Forum Line	n.a.
Rothmans Tobacco Company Ltd.	42
Samoa Forest Corporation	103
Samoa Iron and Steel Fabrication Ltd.	12
Other commercially orientated government agencies	
Broadcasting Department	24
Post and Telecom Department	307
Sub-total [k]	2,644

---

k Excluding enterprises for which employment numbers are unavailable and companies with a minority government shareholding.

Source: Samoan authorities.

Table A3.13: Public enterprises in FSM

	Employees (persons) [a]
National Government	
Bank of FSM	76
FSM Development Bank	39
FSM Telecommunications Corp.	140
Micronesian Longline Fishing Corp.	5
National Fishing Corporation	150
Pacific Island Airfreight	9
FSM Post Office	32
FSM Coconut Development Authority	3
Chuuk State	
Chuuk Coconut Authority	4
Chuuk Department of Transportation: Ports	14
Chuuk Public Utility Corporation	95
Chuuk Housing Authority	15
Kosrae State Government	
Kosrae Broadcast Station	5
Kosrae Department of Transport and Utility/Ports	8
Kosrae Department of Transport and Utility/Water	2
Kosrae Utility Authority	33
Pacific Tuna Industries	25
Micronesian Petroleum Corp.	
Pohnpei State Government	
Pohnpei Broiler Project	5
Pohnpei Economic Development Authority	70
Pohnpei Fisheries Corp.	72
Pohnpei Port Authority	35
Pohnpei Utility Corp. Electricity	120
Pohnpei Utility Corp. Wtr/Sewer	62
Pohnpei Transport Authority	195
Pohnpei Housing Authority	13
Caroline Fisheries Corporation	58
Yap State Government	
Yap Fishing Authority	31
Yap Transportation Authority	17
Yap State Public Service Corp.	87
Yap Purse Seining Corp.	33
Yap Fishing Corp.	n.a.
Sub-total [b]	1,453

n.a. not available
a Latest estimate, mostly 1995.
b Excluding enterprises for which employment numbers are unavailable and companies with a minority government shareholding.
Source: EMPAT 1997.

Table A3.14: Public enterprises in Tonga

Enterprise	Employees (persons) [a]
Fully government-owned	
International Dateline Hotel Ltd.	106
Post Office Department	47
Royal Tongan Airline Ltd.	85
Tonga Broadcasting Commission	65
Chronicle (newspaper)	12
Tonga Electric Power Board	329
Tonga Investment Ltd.	95
- Frisco	n.a.
- Home Gas	n.a.
- Pili Quarry	n.a.
- Palm Soap	n.a.
- Pacific Warehouse Co. Ltd.	n.a.
- Primary Produce	n.a.
Tonga Telecommunication Commission	287
Tonga Water Board	120
Tonga Development Bank	154
Tonga Timber Ltd.	77
Partially government-owned	
Majority shareholding	
Charity Foundation Trust Ltd.	n.a.
Duty Free Shops Ltd.	22
Sea Star Fishing Company Ltd.	76
Shipping Company of Polynesia Ltd.	183
Minority shareholding	
Air Pacific Ltd.	n.a.
Bank of Tonga	n.a.
International Finance Corporation	n.a.
Pacific Forum Line Ltd.	n.a.
Royal Beer Company Ltd.	n.a.
Sub-total [b]	1,702

n.a. not available
a Latest estimate, mostly 1995.
b Excluding enterprises for which employment numbers are unavailable and companies with a minority government shareholding.
Source: Tongan authorities.

Table A3.15: Public enterprises in the Marshall Islands

Enterprise

Pacific Dairy Plant
Marshalls Energy Company
Air Marshall Islands
Majuro Water and Sewer Company
WSZO Radio Station
National Shipping Agency
Tobolar Copra Processing
Post Office
National Telecommunications Authority
Kwajalein Enterprises
Bank of Marshall Islands

Source: Marshall Islands authorities

A4   IMPLICATIONS

One of the key contributions of this report is a clarification of how the PMCs can improve the quality of their government.   This Annex provides support for the view that the PMC public sectors tend to be unusually large.   The extensive involvement of government in the economy is an important reason why public sector reform should be pursued—even small improvements in the quality of government may have a substantial effect on social welfare, perhaps more so than in most other countries.

Certainly, the extensive government involvement in business is incompatible with the framework for government presented in this report.   The collapse of the Bank of Fiji, the dismal financial performance of many public fishing operations in the region, and the large bailout required of Polynesia Airlines are obvious examples of the downside of government involvement in business.   The typical result of extensive government involvement is the crowding out of a wide spectrum of private sector activity and weak growth.   Considerable resources are allocated to non-core activities and ultimately this must be at the expense of the highest priorities of governments.   A PMC government seeking to

implement the framework of this report must aim to divest itself of many of its public enterprises.

Table A3.16: Public enterprises in Kiribati

Enterprise

Bank of Kiribati Ltd.
Development Bank of Kiribati
Kiribati Insurance Corporation
Kiribati Provident Fund
Public Utility Board
Solar Energy Company Ltd.
Air Kiribati Ltd.
Kiribati Shipping Services Ltd.
Telecom Services Kiribati Ltd.
Telecom Kiribati Ltd.
Kiribati Broadcasting and Publications Authority
Kiribati Housing Corporation
Amms Co. Ltd. [a]
Abamarkoo Trading Ltd. [b]
Kirimati Marine Exports Ltd. [a]
Bobotin Kiribati Ltd. [a]
Kiribati Oil Co. Ltd. [b]
Te Mautari Co. Ltd. [c]
Atoll Seaweed Co. Ltd.
Tarawa Biscuits Co. Ltd.
Betio Shipyard Ltd.
Otintaai Hotel Ltd.
Captain Cook Hotel Ltd.
Kiribati Supplies Co. Ltd. [b]
Atoll Motor Marine Services Company Ltd. [b]
Kiribati Marine Export Ltd. [c]

a Classified as part of the transport and communication sector.
b Involved in trading activities (e.g. retailing, wholesaling).
c Fishing-based operation.
Source: Kiribati authorities.

A PMC politician or public servant immersed in the demands of government may lose sight of the appropriate size of the public sector. But it is important to keep in mind that other countries have found ways to run smaller public sectors. Hence calls to reconsider the size of the public sector in the PMCs are not academic, they are well-founded on the experience of other developing countries.

This is not to trivialize the challenge of reform. Significant hurdles exist, such as the social costs of right-sizing. But international experience suggests that smaller, more effective governments and the associated reorientation from government to private activity is critical to development.

(Note that the following was not included in the References provided with Chapter 2)

REFERENCES

EMPAT (Economic Management Policy Advisory Team) 1997, *Public Enterprise Reform,* Prepared for the Government of the FSM, Draft, April.

PARTICIPATORY DEVELOPMENT: THE CHALLENGE OF INCLUSION

Participation, similar to most aspects of development, takes on a special meaning in the context of the PMCs. The Pacific Island societies are undergoing a process of modernization which juxtaposes rapidly increasing expectations—brought on by recent access to mass communication, particularly tele ision—upon centuries of traditional culture. While many of their perceived needs used to be met via the traditional channels of village chief or, in the small urban areas, local government, new demands for higher standards of living have made these established lines of authority increasingly less able to respond in ways perceived as adequate by the island populations. Yet, given the tradition of depending on local chiefs to varying degrees, on issues such as land allocation, education or environment protection—the paradox of this region is that the people have become somewhat passive in the pursuit of development. To optimize benefits, people need to become architects of their own development.

The stakeholders in the PMCs are already engaged in a variety of activities such as secondary education (the churches), land allocation and maintaining law and order (the Matais in Samoa) or specific social services (the nongovernmental organizations —NGOs). The objective of this chapter is to focus on the question of how to meaningfully include the key stakeholders in the development process. More specifically, how can governments help achieve sustainable development by harnessing the energies of the other stakeholders, i.e. the private sector, the churches, the NGOs and the local community groups? An important corollary of government focus on core functions is the need to include and catalyze the energies of the other stakeholders in carrying out the non-core functions which are essential for sustainable development. The challenge of

inclusion is to ensure that other stakeholders play a supportive role in core functions, carry out commercial activities, and perform a myriad of other tasks that can enrich people's lives.

Participation by the private sector and other stakeholders is now clearly regarded as a vital component of economic development. As the 1997 World Development Report concludes – "Governments are more effective when they listen to businesses and citizens and work in partnership with them in deciding and implementing policy." The logic behind this assertion is self-evident. When people are actively engaged in a task, when they feel that it is their own and hence have "ownership" of it, they are far more apt to garner their energies in such a way as to best meet their needs. Communication is an essential element of participation. Government must listen to the people to understand their needs; similarly, people need to be informed of government objectives and proposals and technological advances in each sector so that they can know how to best operate to their own advantage. For listening, consultation, and participation to be most effective, all segments of a society must take part: public and private, formal and informal. The provision and enhancement of voice, individual and collective, brings the force of social capital to bear on development, such that people, as catalyzed actors, are both greater contributors and recipients of developmental benefits.

Participation can be seen as an institutional issue. The nature and degree of one's involvement in one's own development depends on the formal and informal institutions which channel voice and provide opportunities for the realization of one's aspirations. The range of institutions which govern participation runs from family to community (especially strong in the Pacific Islands), NGOs, the churches, the modern private sector (which provides employment on a larger scale than indigenous small businesses) and government. It also includes the rule of law, regulations concerning property rights, gender, inheritance and the like. Recognizing the complexity of the participation issue and the opaqueness of the institutional fabric of a society from the outside—as well as the innovative nature of the topic of participation as an aspect of development in the countries of the South Pacific—it was thought that the best arbiters of the existing level and the potential for participation would be the people themselves, both the leadership and the population at large.

Stakeholders as Agents of Development

A key objective of this report is to underline the importance of fostering an enabling environment for the greater inclusion of this region's population in the development process. To better understand first, the ways in which this could be achieved and second, the potential for participatory development, three countries, Fiji, Tonga and Samoa, were selected on a pilot basis. Local interviewers in each of the countries assessed people's views on participation in selected issues affecting the quality of their lives: health, education, micro-finance, land leasing and environmental protection. More generally, people were asked to discuss what they felt to be institutional constraints and opportunities for becoming more actively involved with the resolution of their own needs, in a cross-sectoral, generic manner. The objective was to find out how people could intensify their collaboration with government and enhance the development process.

Methodological Approaches. The populations of the three island states were broken down by gender and location (rural/urban). In Tonga and Fiji, the groups were also broken down by age groups and further in Fiji, by ethnicity (indigenous Fijian and Fiji Indian) and pace of development (stagnant and growth) for rural areas. A total of 14 communities (three in Samoa, five in Tonga and six in Fiji) were selected. Nine communities were rural and five urban or, in the case of Fiji, peri-urban. The method used in all areas was conversational interviewing with individuals. In Fiji and Tonga, this was complemented by Participatory Rural Appraisal (PRA), a more visual technique for eliciting perceptions at the community level, particularly with groups. In Fiji and Samoa, sampling was done on a systematic basis, with individual interviews conducted with 62 and 30 traditional and non-traditional leaders in each place, respectively. In Tonga, the PRA sessions were followed up with interviews and focus groups with community committee leaders, church leaders and town officers. An additional 45 key informant interviews were conducted in the villages of Samoa. In the Fijian and Tongan surveys approximately 180 and 150 people, respectively, participated in focus groups using PRA methodology. In Tonga, survey work was limited in reach and time. But it demonstrated the potential for doing further work in participatory assessments which could contribute to policy formulation in the future.

The interview guide, administered in the three countries, was divided according to the topics of concern but also allowed for the free expression of other issues felt to be important by the people. For the leaders, qualitative, open-ended and naturalistic conversational style of interviewing was chosen as most appropriate for treating issues of sensitivity in small, closed societies; quantification was done where possible. The PRA exercises gave the communities the opportunity to analyze their own problems. Given the limited scale of the survey and the novelty of both the methodology and the topic of participation, the findings presented below are to be taken as more indicative and exploratory than definitive.

Working with Government. While the objective of this assessment was to gauge the potential for participation of the people of the

PMCs, government was always envisaged as a partner in this quest. Inclusion, in this sense, was not just at the level of the people but also implied working with the governments, providing public officials with feedback from their own populations about how the challenge of development could be shared between public and private bodies, incorporating those with and without voice in the system. The Governments in Fiji, Tonga and Samoa were supportive of this initiative as they saw the relevance of participation to their own country's development. And each offered experienced researchers as interviewers. In Fiji and Samoa these interviewers worked under the leadership of local, nongovernmental personnel. In Tonga this work was coordinated by the Prime Minister's Office, via elected local government officials.

Findings. For the interview guide, the choice of issues for this participatory inquiry was made on an *a priori* basis not altogether in keeping with the inductive spirit of the exercise. Not included were issues which appeared to affect largely the urban population of Fiji: housing, infrastructure and social problems (alcohol and kava abuse, domestic violence, insecurity, etc.). The PRA sessions were open-ended to encourage communities to express their priorities and to gain a deeper understanding of the informal and formal institutional mechanisms used for making their voices heard.

Table 4.1 shows the priorities of the different communities in Fiji: rural Fijian (growth and stagnant), rural Fiji Indian, urban Fijian and Fiji Indian and mixed—all divided by gender and, for the Fijian population, by age as well (the Fiji Indian population was considered to be more homogeneous across age lines than the Fijian). Nevertheless, despite this caveat regarding the urban population of Fiji, the selected issues— health, education, micro-finance and land leasing—were among the most important issues of concern for the peoples of all three island-states. Table 4.1 below presents an overview of how the six communities ranked their problems

in the Participatory Policy Research exercise using PRA.

Health. A problem which appears to be general to the PMCs is that of the poor, or inadequate, quality of transmission of public health dissemination. The 1994 World Bank report on health in the PMCs noted that no government in the region had introduced policies and programs capable of altering public behavior. This report went on to recommend increased budget allocations for proactive public health campaigns in the member countries, with the active involvement of women's committees and traditional healers. The majority of the leaders interviewed in Fiji who responded to this issue (24 of 32) stated that public health dissemination was either poor (five) or needed improvement (24). In Samoa, over half (60 percent) of the key informants stated that they learned what they knew about health through their everyday interactions with peers and acquaintances; another 20 percent acquired their health knowledge during their school years. The problem in Fiji was largely erratic transmission of public health services (overly short information campaigns, infrequent visits of public health officials to rural areas). Transmission was often further limited with a majority of information being in English.

In Samoa, two problems emerged: the absence of effective communication regarding health issues from the government, particularly regarding waste management (sewage) because of its associated health risks and illnesses, and suicide, considered to be relatively high. Access to health services was not considered a problem by most (80 percent) of the persons interviewed in Samoa, though it was in the larger country of Fiji, where fully 70 percent of the respondents stated that access was poor. Health services in Fiji clearly suffer from an urban bias, with few resources and no incentive structure to motivate doctors to spend time in rural areas. Again, the quality of health is seen in markedly different ways by the residents of Samoa and Fiji. Among the former, most are satisfied, while a clear majority in Fiji either rated the quality as poor (40 percent) or as needing improvement (44 percent). In Tonga and Fiji one of the main messages was that the high cost of medicine restricted poor people's access to health care. The people of Fiji, similar to those of many poor areas of the world, also complained of insufficient health personnel and the "unhelpful attitude" of health workers towards patients. In Fiji, many doctors are expatriates which sometimes leads to communication difficulties.

Education. The only prevailing critique of the education system that may be said to apply across all of the island-states of the South Pacific is that, for many, the cost is high. In Samoa, this financial burden was supported by the people with little complaint due to the high value they place on education. Nevertheless, most of the people interviewed in all three countries did feel that a closer collaboration between church and state in the provision of education would lower cost and improve quality, particularly in secondary schools, and should be a matter of policy reform. The Fijians, again, were those who voiced the most complaints about their education system. Close to 90 percent of the leaders interviewed stated that the quality of the curriculum and adequacy of resources for education was either poor (31 percent) or needed improvement (58 percent). A major message emerging from Tonga and Fiji was that the curriculum was criticized as being overly academic, and not providing the appropriate skills needed for the workplace.

As with health (above), the rural schools of Fiji appear to also suffer from an urban bias with poor transport to rural schools and no incentives for qualified teachers to go to rural areas (high rents, poor accommodation and isolation were mentioned). The resulting disparity in the quality of education between rural and urban areas was seen by many as a cause for the gradual drift of persons from country to city. In both Tonga and, to a greater extent, in Fiji, people had migrated from the outer islands and formed squatter settlements. One of the main

motivations for this migration was better education for children, illustrating the high value placed on education.

Microfinance. As with poor people everywhere, the people of the PMCs need more access to finance than they presently have. Most of the persons interviewed for this assessment stated that the private banking system was not responsive to their needs, requiring excessive paperwork and collateral for loans, the latter being particularly onerous for those persons in Fiji who were not landowners, but rather lessees (rural Indians) or squatters (urban poor). Some of the problems in accessing credit in Fiji are illustrated. Women felt particularly excluded in Fiji and stated that microfinance was usually "men's talk." Particularly problematic for the Fijians was the perceived low willingness of banks to provide loans for communal projects (sea wall, village flush toilets, etc.) when the Government requires one third of the cost of any communal improvement to be provided by the village as counterpart to the receipt of public funds. Generally, there was a strong widespread feeling that the involvement of NGOs in the microcredit area would facilitate the access and delivery of finance to the people of these countries. The emphasis in many of these societies is on the community as opposed to the individual. People were, therefore, more in favor of NGOs helping assess, secure and monitor loans for groups and communities. Close to two thirds (63 percent) of the respondents in Samoa stated that NGOs should be used as conduits or brokers for monetary loans. They saw the intermediation of the NGOs in the area of microcredit as leading to faster and simpler processing of loans, less collateral requirements and lower interest rates.

Land Leasing. The issue of land leasing is most resonant in Fiji. In Samoa only 20 percent of the interviewees stated that they had ever been lessees; most Samoans have little understanding or interest in leasing, viewing it, dimly, as overly expensive for their limited means and of possible use only in Apia, the major urban area of the country. In Fiji, on the other hand, where leases are widespread and tenuous as regards their security, the issue of land leasing is a major cause for insecurity and racial strife—most of the landowners being Fijian, the lessees Fiji Indian. Perhaps the most important finding of this assessment regarding land leasing is that the institutional structure set in place by the Fiji Government to resolve land leasing issues is not perceived as up to the task by the people of Fiji. The Native Land Trust Board (NLTB) is seen as overly bureaucratic, unresponsive to the demands of the commercial environment; ALTA is seen as too autocratic by landowners. Land leasing generally appears to offer the potential for NGO intermediation as brokers in engaging landowners and lessees in constructive dialogue which can resolve issues on their own terms with more relevance and immediacy than is being done by distant, government agencies. This issue, similar to microfinance (above) points to the need for greater participation between the public and nongovernmental sectors, particularly (re: land) in Fiji.

Environmental Protection. Of all the issues discussed with the people of the islands, environment was the one about which they (a) had the least awareness and (b) saw the least role for themselves as participants. In Samoa, the people did appreciate a certain responsibility, with the young men protecting the coastal areas and mangroves under the direction of the village chiefs (matai). However, in all three countries, there appeared to be little concern regarding any spoilage or destruction of the coastal areas. Only 10 percent of the Samoans interviewed mentioned the importance of guarding against the deposit of litter and using the beach as alternative lavatories. And in Fiji, the general finding was that most communities felt there was no environmental problem at all in their village, despite recorded environmental degradation in many parts of the country. The general need throughout the PMCs is for greater awareness-building of the threats to the environment and what might be done by the active involvement of the area's citizenry in countering these. One fruitful area mentioned as a possible target of opportunity for environmental protection in both Fiji and Samoa was tourism, either via eco-tourism or the levying of fees on tourists for environmental enhancement activities. This is clearly another area where the participation of NGOs would be beneficial.

Effective Participation in Development. The people's voice, as heard in the interviews and focus groups conducted during this brief assessment in Fiji, Tonga and Samoa, expresses a desire for greater involvement in the activities which are perceived as affecting their lives, primarily the basic needs of health and education and that of increased access to credit at reasonable terms. In Fiji, people want to have increased say in the way that land affairs, particularly leasing, is conducted. Environment, while recognized as an issue of importance, is not widely seen as a problem or as an area where popular participation can or should come into play. In each of these issues, though to differing degrees, and transcending all of them, is a perceived blockage of expression beyond the village. Government institutions are seen as remote and top-down; traditional village and community leadership is seen as authoritarian and far less responsive to individual than to community needs. These factors are important if participation is to be viewed in the unique cultural context of the Pacific Islands where the emphasis is on groups as opposed to individuals. In Tonga, town and district officers often find it difficult to voice the priorities of their communities to the policy maker because of the top-down communication flow and hierarchical system of government. In addition, many of the officers have to supplement their incomes and therefore have less time to carry out their roles as people's representatives. The complex institutional frameworks exist in villages for all three islands where information can flow effectively. The opening of effective channels for voice and participation through the increased engagement of nongovernmental institutions, as well as strengthening local government, is clearly a priority for the sound and sustainable development of the island states of the South Pacific.

While it is not the intention of the report to prescribe specific measures of policy reform, there are certain activities which would follow naturally from the insights gleaned above. One clear need throughout the PMCs covered in this survey was for more effective, penetrating public information campaigns. This need was found to be especially evident in public health and environmental protection. Similarly, technical expertise and professional guidance in the basic needs of health and education was found to be sorely lacking in the rural areas of Fiji; one would expect that this need for more effective outreach would also be felt in the more remote outer islands of many of the PMCs. Consideration should be given to incentives for professionals to spend time in these more remote places as well as to the training of para-professionals from these outlying communities who could better serve their own populations with no need for displacement.

More generally, in each of the countries surveyed and, throughout the region, there is a lack of effective communication between the various centers of leadership. Traditional local chiefs (matais in Samoa, turagas in Fiji), while sometimes also being government officials, seemed as a group to be at odds, (even confrontational, in Samoa), with elected government. The NGO community, which could and should be harnessed to serve the interests of the countries' populations, especially the poor, often appeared remote. The potential for NGO involvement in building public awareness around environmental and health concerns, in facilitating access and procedures for microcredit, and in the intermediation of land disputes (particularly in Fiji) was one clear target of opportunity signaled by this systematic listening to the people of the South Pacific.

Beyond the particular findings of the survey conducted in the three PMCs, the emerging lesson of this work is that there is both a need and a feasibility of giving voice and enhancing the participation of the peoples of this remote island-studded region. The governments which were approached concerning their interest in participation were open and cooperative, aware of the developmental importance of this topic. The people and leaders in villages and towns also showed themselves to be willing interlocutors in this process, giving many hours of their precious time to the individual interviews and focus group discussions.

Two primary methods of inquiry were chosen, beneficiary assessment (BA) and Participatory Rural Appraisal (PRA). Each was found effective. Others could also be used to gain a fuller understanding of the potential for participatory development. The work presented here demonstrates that there are ways for these island states to draw upon the vast reserves of energy of their own people and institutions so as to develop not only from increased external ties but also from within, from the social capital embedded in their own rich cultures as adapted to the needs and opportunities of a modernizing world.

Table A4.1: Perceived Rankings

	Rural								Urban						
	Indigenous Fijian (moderate growth)			Fijian (low growth)			Fiji-Indian		Fiji-Indian		Indigenous Fijian			Mixed	
Rank	M	F	Y	M	F	Y	M	F	M	F	M	F	Y	M	F
1	9	9	8	9	5	9	4	9	4	11	4	11	4	11	5
2	4	7	5	4	8	10	9	5	11	11	9	10	9	2	2
3	6	11	10	2	7	11	3	8	11	10	6	9	11	8	8
4	1	8	11	10	11	6	11	10	8	6	11	10	4	9	8
5			7	1	2	8	4	11	9	11	10	5	5		9

Key
M = Males   F = Females   Y = Youth
1. Population increase 2. Social problems 3. Crime 4. Land leasing 5. Education 6. Micro finance 7. Environment 8. Health 9. Employment 10. Housing 11. Infrastructure

THE STATE OF THE ENVIRONMENT IN THE PMCS

The PMCs are characterized by large sea areas, small populations and little industrial activity. These characteristics help limit and localize water pollution problems and make major air pollution unlikely. Marine resources are generally in good condition, although over-fishing and reef degradation is common near major population centers. The primary environmental problems arise from the small land area combined with an emphasis on agriculture and, for some PMCs, logging. This gives rise to waste management problems in heavily populated areas and land degradation through land clearing.

All PMCs face major waste management problems. Solid waste disposal is particularly difficult in the smaller islands due to a shortage or absence of landfill sites. Poor or absent sewerage systems give rise to localized water pollution problems; lagoon areas with poor tidal flushing are the worst affected. Most PMCs see the possibility for sea level rise from climate change as an important long term problem, given the extent of coastal living and in some cases, very low heights above sea level.

Table A5.1: A Stock-Take of Environmental Problems

	Fiji	Kiribati	FSM	Marshall Is.	Solomon Is.	Tonga	Vanuatu	Samoa
LAND AND SEA								
Deforestation	x		x		x	x	x	x
- agrodeforestation	x	x	x	x		x		
Land degradation	x	x	x	x	x	x	x	x
- soil erosion	x		x		x	x	x	x
Depletion of oceanic/coastal resources	x	x	x	x	x	x	x	x
- offshore migratory fish stocks								
- inshore and lagoon marine resources	x	x	x	x	x	x	x	x
- reef degradation	x	x	x	x	x	x	x	x
- coastal erosion	x	x	x	x	x	x		x
- mangrove destruction	x	x		x	x	x		x
Marine pollution	x	x	x	x	x	x	x	x
- land-based	x	x	x	x	x	x	x	x
- sea-based			x					
Loss of biodiversity	x	x	x		x	x	x	x
- loss of species/ecosystems	x	x	x		x	x	x	x
- lack of protected areas	x	x	x		x	x		
FRESH WATER								
Water quantity		x		x		x		
Water quality	x	x	x		x	x		
- surface water	x		x				x	x
- underground water/freshwater lens		x	x			x	x	x
AIR AND CLIMATE								
Air pollution	x							
Climate change/sea level rise	x	x	x	x	x	x		x
WASTE								
Waste management	x	x	x	x	x	x	x	x
- solid urban waste	x	x	x	x	x	x		x
- liquid urban waste	x	x		x	x	x	x	x
ENERGY RESOURCES		x				x	x	x
Urban fuelwood shortages		x	x	x		x	x	x
SOCIAL/DEMOGRAPHIC ISSUES								
Population growth		x	x	x	x		x	
Health hazard	x	x		x	x			
Poverty	x					x		

Note: A x indicates the presence of a significant environment problem.
Source: SPREP 1996.

RELATIONSHIP BETWEEN FOREIGN AID AND GOVERNMENT EXPENDITURE

Objective:

The Pacific Island economies have been amongst the highest recipients of foreign aid in per capita terms. Aid programs have financed both development expenditure as well as current expenditure of governments. The proposed hypothesis is that there is a strong relationship between aid flows and government expenditure. More specifically, the aim of this analysis is to test the following relationships:

(i) Total government expenditure as a function of foreign aid and GNP per capita.

(ii) Current government expenditure as a function of foreign aid and GNP per capita.

Specification of the Model:

Equation (1): $Y = \alpha_0 + \alpha_1 X_1 + \alpha_2 X_2 + \varepsilon$
where Y = total government expenditure as a percentage of GDP, X_1 = aid as a percentage of GDP, X_2 = GNP per capita, and ε = error term, α_0 = intercept, and α_1 and α_2 are the coefficients.

Equation (2): $Y = \beta_0 + \beta_1 X_1 + \beta_2 X_2 + \varepsilon$
where Y = Current expenditure as a percentage of GDP, X_1 = aid as a percentage of GDP, X_2 = GNP per capita, and ε = error term, β_0 = intercept, and β_1 and β_2 are the coefficients.

Equation (1a): $Y = \alpha_0 + \alpha_1 X_1 + \alpha_2 X_2 + \alpha_3 X_3 + \varepsilon$
where Y = total government expenditure as a percentage of GDP, X_1 = aid as a percentage of GDP, X_2 = GNP per capita, X_3 = square of GNP per capita, and ε = error term, α_0 = intercept, and α_1, α_2 and α_3 are the coefficients.

Equation (2a): $Y = \beta_0 + \beta_1 X_1 + \beta_2 X_2 + \beta_3 X_3 + \varepsilon$

where Y = current expenditure as a percentage of GDP, X_1 = aid as a percentage of GDP, X_2 = GNP per capita, X_3 = square of GNP per capita, and ε = error term, β_0 = intercept, and β_1 and β_2 are the coefficients.

Data Set:

Pooled time series–cross section data for eight Pacific Islands countries (Fiji, Kiribati, FSM, Marshall Islands, Samoa, Solomon Islands, Tonga, Vanuatu) during 1990-96. Some data were missing. Total number of observations used was 49.

Results:

Equation	Intercept	X_1 Aid/GDP	X_2 GNP Per Capita	X_3 GNP Per Capita Squared	Adjusted R^2	F Statistic
				Table 1: Government Expenditure as a Function of Foreign Aid and Per Capita Income		
(1)	51.60 (10.03)	1.28 (13.89)	-0.013 (-4.09)		0.82	107.18
(2)	20.66 (4.93)	0.89 (11.86)	0.0001 (-0.05)		0.74	70.47
(1a)	77.01 (5.01)	1.32 (14.15)	-0.05 (-2.30)	1.38×10^{-5} (1.75)	0.82	75.68
(2a)	38.40 (3.04)	0.92 (11.97)	-0.03 (-1.48)	6.48×10^{-6} (1.48)	0.75	48.95

Note 1: T- statistics are in parentheses ( ).

Conclusions:

(1)   The coefficients of X_1 are highly significant in all four equations (high T-values), indicative of a strong relationship between government expenditure and aid flows.

(2)   The coefficients of X_2 are highly significant in equations (1) and (1a), indicating that as GNP per capita increases total expenditure as a proportion of GDP is likely to decline, with a likely increasing role for the private sector. In equation (2), the coefficient of X_2 is not significant, indicative of a weak association between government current expenditure and GNP per capita.

(3)   The coefficients of X_3 are small in equations (1a) and (2a), but significant, indicative of a slight non-linear relationship between government expenditure and GNP per capita.

(4)   The relatively high adjusted R^2 and the F Statistic point to a strong explanatory power of the model.

STATISTICAL APPENDIX

ON

PUBLIC FINANCE

Table 3.1: Central Government Revenue 1/

(In percent of GDP)

	1985-89 2/	1990	1991	1992	1993	1994	1995	1996	Av. 1990-95
Fiji	24.0	28.1	27.4	25.7	25.7	26.1	25.9	25.1	26.5
Kiribati 3/	46.4	49.3	57.0	94.3	100.9	87.3	87.8	60.9	79.4
FSM 4/	21.5	27.2	30.0	32.2	31.6	29.4	27.9	...	29.7
Marshall Islands	20.0	32.9	33.6	31.3	33.1	30.1	29.8	...	31.8
Samoa	40.2	37.3	41.9	42.5	45.6	43.6	39.7	40.7	41.8
Solomon Islands 5/	23.4	28.5	28.8	33.0	26.7	28.7	28.6	25.5	29.0
Tonga	27.4	27.6	26.9	24.4	25.6	26.0	27.0	25.5	26.3
Vanuatu	25.8	26.5	23.1	23.5	21.5	23.8	24.2	...	23.8

Source: Official Documents; World Bank Regional Economic Reports, Public Expenditure Review and Country Economic Memoranda; IMF Staff Reports and Recent Economic Development Reports.
1/ All ratios are for FY ending in specified calendar year.
2/ For FSM and Marshall Islands, covers FY 1986-89; for Solomon Islands 1985-88;
   for Tonga, 1985-88; for Vanuatu 1985-87.
3/ From 1992, includes all revenue acrued to the RERF.
4/ Includes the General Government.
5/ From 1990, GDP was revised downward. This accounts for the increase in revenue/GDP ratio.

Table 3.2: External Grants to PMC Governments 1/

(In percent of GDP)

	Av. 1985-89	1990	1991	1992	1993	1994	1995	1996	Av. 1990-95
Fiji	0.9	0.4	0.4	0.3	0.2	0.2	0.2	0.2	0.3
Kiribati	36.7	46.3	38.4	58.3	41.6	32.7	18.4	19.2	39.3
FSM	78.3	76.3	69.8	57.1	51.8	51.4	52	...	59.7
Marshall Islands	49.1	71.4	60.9	55	52.5	46.3	44.9	...	55.2
Samoa	15.6	13.2	8.1	13.5	15.3	10.5	19.8	21.7	13.4
Solomon Islands	7.6	5.1	19.4	17.6	14.5	18.4	12.6	12.5	14.6
Tonga	17.8	15.8	10.1	13.7	16.6	14.8	16.4	12.8	14.6
Vanuatu	25.8	17.6	16.6	14.3	12.4	13.4	13.3	...	14.6

Source: Official Documents; World Bank Regional Economic Reports, Public Expenditure Review and Country Economic Memoranda; IMF Staff Reports and Recent Economic Development Reports.
1/ See table 3.1. footnotes 1, 2 and 4.

Table 3.3: Government External Borrowing, Net 1/

(in percent of GDP)

	Av. 1985-89	1990	1991	1992	1993	1994	1995	1996	Av. 1990-95
Fiji	-0.5	-0.5	-1.0	-0.6	-0.5	0.3	-0.1	-0.1	-0.4
Kiribati	...	...	...	...	...	...	...	...	...
FSM	-0.2	9.3	52.1	9.9	10.6	-3.8	-4.3	...	12.3
Marshall Islands	9.3	47.3	54.3	8.2	13.6	23.2	-12.0	...	22.4
Samoa	2.1	8.7	16.6	11.6	14.3	12.0	3.3	1.3	11.1
Solon on Islands	6.7	6.2	-0.8	2.7	0.4	0.7	1.0	-0.3	1.7
Tonga	2.3	1.9	0.9	1.1	1.4	1.6	3.6	2.2	1.8
Vanuatu	1.5	...	2.5	3.1	0.3	0.5	0.2	...	1.1

Source: Official Documents; World Bank Regional Economic Reports, Public Expenditure Review and Country Economic Memoranda; IMF Staff Reports and Recent Economic Development Reports.
1/ See table 3.1 footnotes 1, 2 and 4.

Table 3.4: Government Borrowing From Domestic Banks 1/

(In percent of GDP)

	Av. 1985-89	1990	1991	1992	1993	1994	1995	1996	Av. 1990-95
Fiji	0.8	-0.4	1.2	1.2	-0.1	-1.3	-0.3	...	0.0
Kiribati	...	0.0	0.0	0.0	0.0	0.0	0.0	...	0.0
FSM	0.0	0.0	0.0	0.0	0.0	0.0	0.0	0.0	0.0
Marshall Islands	0.0	0.0	0.0	0.0	0.0	0.0	0.0	0.0	0.0
Samoa	-6.8	-4.9	-8.7	2.9	7.0	1.0	5.2	-3.8	0.4
Solomon Islands	0.7	2.9	11.9	2.0	4.7	4.7	1.1	...	4.5
Tonga	-1.4	-4.5	0.3	2.7	-2.6	-2.7	-0.1	1.0	-1.2
Vanuatu	-13.1	-7.8	-1.5	0.3	0.8	1.2	1.4	...	-0.9

Source: Official Documents; World Bank Regional Economic Reports, Public Expenditure Review and Country Economic Memoranda; IMF Staff Reports and Recent Economic Development Reports.
1/ See table 3.1 footnotes 1, 2 and 4.

Table 3.5: Government Borrowing from Domestic Nonbanks 1/

(In percent of GDP)

	Av. 1985-89	1990	1991	1992	1993	1994	1995	1996	Av. 1990-95
Fiji	2.9	0.6	1.3	2.4	4.1	2.5	0.9	...	1.9
Kiribati	0.0	0.0	0.0	0.0	0.0	0.0	0.0	0	0.0
FSM	...	0.0	0.0	0.0	0.0	0.0	0.0	0	0.0
Marshall Islands	...	...	...	...	...	...	...	...	0.0
Samoa	1.4	-0.4	3.2	2.0	0.5	-1.2	0.7	0.8	0.8
Solomon Islands	0.3	-2.2	2.0	2.5	2.8	1.3	2.3	...	1.4
Tonga	-0.5	...	...	2.6	-2.0	-3.7	-3.5	-2.8	-1.1
Vanuatu	1.1	...	0.5	0.0	0.2	1.4	0.0	...	0.3

Source: Official Documents; World Bank Regional Economic Reports, Public Expenditure Review and Country Economic Memoranda; IMF Staff Reports and Recent Economic Development Reports.
1/ See table 3.1 footnotes 1, 2 and 4.

Table 3.6: Central Government Current Expenditure 1/

(In percent of GDP)

	Av. 1985-89	1990	1991	1992	1993	1994	1995	1996	Av. 1990-95
Fiji	23.0	23.3	23.5	24.5	25.6	23.8	23.5	23.3	24.0
Kiribati	46.8	53.5	56.7	56.2	54.9	56.9	68.7	63.1	57.8
FSM	64.8	62.8	69.9	67.8	66.6	65.8	64.7	...	66.3
Marshall Islands	48.9	70.1	79.8	81.8	78.4	64.1	58.7	32.7	72.2
Samoa 2/	21.3	20.5	23.9	42.5	42.4	42.0	30.8		33.7
Solomon Islands	26.1	34.4	38.0	36.0	30.3	31.3	29.2	28.8	33.2
Tonga	24.9	27.8	28.6	25.4	23.8	22.0	23.1	24.1	25.1
Vanuatu	36.1	35.1	28.9	27.9	26.5	26.6	26.3	...	28.6

Source: Official Documents; World Bank Regional Economic Reports, Public Expenditure Review and Country Economic Memoranda; IMF Staff Reports and Recent Economic Development Reports.
1/ See table 3.1 footnotes 1, 2 and 4.
2/ Expenditure data were reclassified from 1992, when expenditure previously reported as domestically financed development expenditure were moved to the current budget.

Table 3.7: Government Current Account Balance, Excluding Grants 1/

(In percent of GDP)

	Av. 1985-89	1990	1991	1992	1993	1994	1995	1996	Av. 1990-95
Fiji	1.0	4.8	3.9	1.2	0.1	2.3	2.4	2	2.5
Kiribati 1/	-0.4	-4.2	0.3	38.1	46.0	30.4	19.1	-2.2	21.6
FSM	-43.3	-35.6	-39.9	-35.6	-35.0	-36.4	-36.8	...	-36.6
Marshall Islands	-28.9	-37.2	-46.2	-50.5	-45.3	-34.0	-28.9	...	-40.4
Samoa 2/	18.9	16.8	18.0	0.0	3.2	1.6	8.9	8	8.1
Solomon Islands	-2.7	-5.9	-9.2	-3.0	-3.6	-2.6	-0.6	-2.3	-4.2
Tonga	2.5	-0.2	-1.7	-1.0	1.8	4.0	3.9	2.5	1.1
Vanuatu	-10.3	-8.6	-5.8	-4.4	-5.0	-2.8	-2.1	...	-4.8

Source: Tables 3.1 and 3.6.
1/ See table 3.1 footnotes 1, 2 and 4.
1/ From 1992, includes all revenue accrued to RERF.
2/ See footnote 1, table 3.6.

Table 3.8: Government Development Expenditure 1/

(In percent of GDP)

	Av. 1985-89	1990	1991	1992	1993	1994	1995	1996	Av. 1990-95
Fiji	5.0	4.9	5.7	4.5	3.7	4.0	3.1	7.3	3.5
Kiribati	37.8	49.3	40.1	62.2	44.5	38.5	24.3	24.2	34.9
FSM	18.2	36.9	37.9	26.8	20.1	15.6	13.6	...	19.0
Marshall Islands	13.2	32.4	21.5	30.8	21.2	25.8	28.5	...	21.3
Samoa 2/	31.2	31.1	36.0	30.0	40.5	23.6	38.3	27.8	28.1
Solomon Islands	12.6	6.1	23.5	21.8	18.8	22.4	14.4	14.2	16.8
Tonga	20.9	22.9	18.5	19.3	16.6	16.3	23.5	19.2	15.7
Vanuatu	17.8	19.1	12.4	13.2	8.8	13.6	12.8	...	10.1

Source: Official Documents; World Bank Regional Economic Reports, Public Expenditure Review and Country Economic Memoranda; IMF Staff Reports and Recent Economic Development Reports.
1/ See table 3.1 footnotes 1, 2 and 4.
2/ See Table 3.6 footnote 1.

Table 3.9: Total Government Expenditure 1/

(In percent of GDP)

	Av. 1985-89	1990	1991	1992	1993	1994	1995	1996	Av. 1990-95
Fiji	28.0	28.2	29.2	29.0	29.3	27.8	26.6	30.0	28.4
Kiribati	84.6	102.7	96.8	118.4	99.4	95.4	93.0	87.3	100.6
FSM	83.0	99.7	107.8	94.6	86.7	81.4	78.3	...	89.8
Marshall Islands	62.1	102.5	101.3	112.6	99.6	89.9	87.2	...	98.1
Samoa	52.5	51.6	59.9	72.5	82.9	65.6	69.1	80.5	70.0
Solomon Islands	38.7	40.5	61.5	57.8	49.1	53.7	43.6	43	53.1
Tonga	45.8	50.7	47.1	44.7	40.4	38.3	46.6	43.3	43.4
Vanuatu	53.9	54.2	41.3	41.1	35.3	40.2	39.1	...	39.4

Source: Tables 3.6 and 3.8.
1/ See table 3.1 footnotes 1,2 and 4.

Table 3.10: Government Overall Balance, Including Grants 1/

(In percent of GDP)

	Av. 1985-89	1990	1991	1992	1993	1994	1995	1996	Av. 1990-95
Fiji	-3.1	0.3	-1.4	-3.0	-3.4	-1.5	-0.5	-0.5	-1.6
Kiribati	-1.5	-7.2	-1.4	34.2	43.1	24.6	13.2	13.2	17.8
FSM	16.8	3.8	-8.0	-5.3	-3.3	-0.6	1.6	1.5	-2.0
Marshall Islands	7.0	1.8	-6.8	-26.3	-14.0	-13.5	-12.5	-12.5	-11.9
Samoa	3.3	-1.1	-9.9	-16.5	-22.0	-11.5	-9.6	9.5	-11.8
Solomon Islands	-7.7	-6.9	-13.3	-7.2	-7.9	-6.6	-2.4	-2.4	-7.4
Tonga	-0.6	-7.3	-10.1	-6.6	1.8	2.5	-3.2	-3.2	-3.8
Vanuatu	-2.3	-10.1	-1.6	-3.3	-1.4	-3.0	-1.6	-1.5	-3.5

Source: Tables 3.2 and 3.11.
1/ See table 3.1 footnotes 1, 2, 3 and 4.

Table 3.11: Government Overall Balance, Excluding Grants 1/

(In percent of GDP)

	Av. 1985-89	1990	1991	1992	1993	1994	1995	1996	Av. 1990-95
Fiji	-4.0	-0.1	-1.8	-3.3	-3.6	-1.7	-0.7	-4.9	-1.9
Kiribati	-38.2	-53.4	-39.7	-24.1	1.5	-8.1	-5.2	-25.4	-21.5
FSM	-61.5	-72.5	-77.8	-62.4	-55.1	-52.0	-50.4	...	-61.7
Marshall Islands	-42.1	-69.6	-67.7	-81.3	-66.5	-59.8	-57.4	...	-67.1
Samoa	-12.3	-14.3	-18.0	-30.0	-37.3	-22.0	-29.4	-19.8	-25.2
Solomon Islands	-15.3	-12.0	-32.7	-24.8	-22.4	-25.0	-15.0	-16.5	-22.0
Tonga	-18.4	-23.1	-20.2	-20.3	-14.8	-12.3	-19.6	-16.7	-18.4
Vanuatu	-28.1	-27.7	-18.2	-17.6	-13.8	-16.4	-14.9	...	-18.1

Source: Tables 3.7 and 3.8.
1/ See table 3.1 footnotes 1, 2, 3 and 4.

Table 3.12: Government Expenditure on Wages and Salaries 1/

(In percent of GDP)

	Av. 1985-8	1990	1991	1992	1993	1994	1995	1996	Av. 1990-95
Fiji	12.2	12.0	12.3	12.3	12.0	11.7	11.4	11.2	12.0
Kiribati	18.6	20.3	22.2	23.2	23.1	21.3	26.0	25.9	22.7
FSM	30.6	30.3	30.3	30.2	29.7	28.4	29.4	...	29.7
Marshall Islands	15.2	22.5	24.5	24.2	22.8	22.7	21.5	...	23.0
Samoa	11.0	...	...	13.0	13.2	13.4	11.7	10.8	8.5
Solomon Islands	12.0	14.6	16.2	14.3	12.5	12.6	10.9	10.8	13.5
Tonga	...	...	12.8	13.2	11.2	11.6	12.2	13	10.2
Vanuatu	15.6	13.1	12.6	12.6	11.9	11.5	11.9	...	12.3

Source: Official Documents; World Bank Regional Economic Reports, Public Expenditure Review and Country Economic Memoranda; IMF Staff Reports and Recent Economic Development Reports.
1/ See table 3.1 footnotes 1, 2 and 4.

Table 3.13: Government Expenditure on Interest Payments 1/

(In percent of GDP)

	Av. 1985-89	1990	1991	1992	1993	1994	1995	1996	Av. 1990-95
Fiji	3.6	4.1	3.5	3.1	3.0	2.9	3.1	2.9	3.3
Kiribati	...	...	...	0.1	0.1	0.1	0.2	0.2	0.1
FSM	0.0	0.0	0.0	2.8	3.5	2.7	2.3	...	1.9
Marshall Islands	7.8	9.4	8.2	12.3	12.0	7.1	5.9	...	9.2
Samoa	2.8	...	...	1.9	1.7	1.6	1.3	...	1.1
Solomon Islands	2.2	4.2	5.5	4.3	3.9	4.1	4.1	3	4.3
Tonga	...	...	...	...	...	...	...	...	0.0
Vanuatu	1.4	2.3	0.9	1.0	0.8	0.7	0.7		1.1

Source: Official Documents; World Bank Regional Economic Reports, Public Expenditure Review and Country Economic Memoranda; IMF Staff Reports and Recent Economic Development Reports.
1/ See table 3.1 footnotes 1, 2 and 4.

Table 3.14: Government Expenditure on Public Administration

(In percent of GDP)

	1990	1991	1992	1993	1994	1995	1996
Fiji	5.7	5.6	6.0	6.3	5.7	5.6	5.6
Kiribati	16.8	20.3	18.3	18.0	19.5	22.1	21.5
FSM	...	...	...	...	...	...	...
Marshall Islands	...	...	...	...	...	...	...
Samoa	...	...	10.0	9.0	9.3	7.3	8.6
Solomon Islands	...	...	...	...	...	...	...
Tonga	13.2	10.6	9.8	8.7	8.1	9.0	9.6
Vanuatu	...	7.7	8.2	8.5	9.7	10.6	...

Table 3.15: Government Current Expenditure on Law and Order

(In percent of GDP)

	1990	1991	1992	1993	1994	1995	1996	Av. 1990-95
Fiji	3.4	3.3	3.2	2.9	3.0	2.9	2.9	3.1
Kiribati	...	...	...	...	...	...	...	...
FSM	...	...	...	...	...	...	...	...
Marshall Islands	...	...	...	...	...	...	...	...
Samoa	...	...	2.1	1.9	1.9	1.6	1.8	1.2
Solomon Islands	...	...	...	...	...	...	...	...
Tonga	...	3.0	3.1	2.8	2.7	3.1	3.1	2.4
Vanuatu	...	1.8	1.8	2.0	2.5	2.2	...	1.7

Source: Official Documents; World Bank Regional Economic Reports, Public Expenditure Review and Country Economic Memoranda; IMF Staff Reports and Recent Economic Development Reports.
1/ See table 3.1 footnotes 1, 2 and 4.

Table 3.16: Government Current Expenditure on Economic Services

(In percent of GDP)

	1990	1991	1992	1993	1994	1995	1996
Fiji	4.1	4.4	4.9	4.8	4.1	4.0	3.9
Kiribati	20.4	17.8	17.3	16.5	16.5	20.4	16.0
FSM	...	...	...	...	...	...	...
Marshall Islands	...	...	...	...	...	...	...
Samoa	...	...	7.8	6.9	8.0	5.1	5.0
Solomon Islands	...	...	...	...	...	...	...
Tonga	5.5	6.1	5.9	5.4	4.9	4.9	5.0
Vanuatu	...	3.7	3.7	3.3	2.6	2.7	...

Source: Official Documents; World Bank Regional Economic Reports, Public Expenditure Review and Country Economic Memoranda; IMF Staff Reports and Recent Economic Development Reports.
1/ See table 3.1 footnotes 1, 2 and 4.

Table 3.17: Government Expenditure on Health

(In percent of GDP)

	1990	1991	1992	1993	1994	1995	1996	1997	Av. 1990-95
Fiji 2/	2.5	2.6	2.9	2.8	2.9	2.7	3.8	3.8	2.8
Kiribati 3/	7.0	8.5	9.3	8.8	9.8	10.8	10.7		9.0
FSM	...	...	...	...	...	...	...		...
Marshall Islands 3/	...	11.6	9.5	6.9	5.4	6.2	...		6.6
Samoa 3/	...	...	4.2	4.3	4.2	3.7	4.1	4.1	2.7
Solomon Islands 3/	...	...	...	...	...	...	2.9		...
Tonga 4/	3.3	3.6	4.3	4.1	3.8	4.2	4.2		3.9
Vanuatu 3/	...	2.4	2.4	2.6	2.0	2.2	...		1.9

Source: Official Documents; World Bank Regional Economic Reports, Public Expenditure Review and Country Economic Memoranda; IMF Staff Reports and Recent Economic Development Reports.
1/ See table 3.1 footnotes 1, 2 and 4.
2/ Current and capital expenditure on health, social welfare, urban development, housing and environment, youth, employment and sports.
3/ Recurrent health expenditure.
4/ Current and capital expenditure on health.

Table 3.18: Government Expenditure on Education 1/

(in percent of GDP)

	1990	1991	1992	1993	1994	1995	1996	1997	Av. 1990-95
Fiji 2/	5.3	5.6	5.5	5.6	5.5	5.4	4.4	4.4	5.5
Kiribati 3/	9.2	10.1	11.3	11.6	11.0	14.1	13.2		11.2
FSM	...	...	...	...	...	...	...		...
Marshall Islands 2/	14.8	11.8	9.5	9.5	10.6	...	...		9.4
Samoa	...	...	5.6	5.5	5.4	4.8	4.5	4.4	3.6
Solomon Islands	...	...	...	...	...	...	4.2		...
Tonga 2/	5.3	7.3	7.9	8.8	8.2	7.3	9.8		7.5
Vanuatu	...	4.6	5.0	4.7	4.9	5.0	...		4.9

Source: Official Documents; World Bank Regional Economic Reports, Public Expenditure Review and Country Economic Memoranda; IMF Staff Reports and Recent Economic Development Reports.
1/ See table 3.1 footnotes 1, 2 and 4.
2/ Current and capital health expenditure.
3/ Recurrent health expenditure.

Table 3.19: Government Current Expenditure for Infrastructure 1/

(In percent of GDP)

	1990	1991	1992	1993	1994	1995	1996	Av. 1990-95
Fiji	2.4	2.7	2.9	2.9	2.4	2.2	2.2	2.9
Kiribati	6.0	6.4	6.6	7.2	6.9	8.8	7.0	6.9
FSM	...	...	...	...	...	...	...	...
Marshall Islands	...	7.2	5.9	5.0	4.3	3.4	...	4.3
Samoa	...	...	4.8	4.6	5.2	3.1	4.7	2.9
Solomon Islands	...	...	...	...	...	...	0.7	...
Tonga	3.5	3.8	3.6	3.1	2.9	2.8	2.8	3.2
Vanuatu	...	...	...	...	...	...	...	...

Source: Official Documents; World Bank Regional Economic Reports, Public Expenditure Review and Country Economic Memoranda; IMF Staff Reports and Recent Economic Development Reports.
1/ See table 3.1 footnotes 1, 2 and 4.

BIBLIOGRAPHY

General

ADB (Asian Development Bank). 1996a. *Strategy for the Pacific: Policies and Programs for Sustainable Growth,* Pacific Studies Series, Manila.

_____. 1996b. *Vanuatu: Economic Performance, Policy and Reform Issues,* Pacific Studies Series, Manila.

_____. 1997c. *Emerging Asia: Changes and Challenges,* Manila.

_____. 1997d. *Improving Growth Prospects in the Pacific,* Manila.

AusAID (Australian Agency for International Development). 1997. *South Pacific Economic and Social Statistics.*

Iqbal, Farrukh (with the assistance of Thorsten Block). 1995. *Working Paper III: The Determinants of Growth in Pacific Island Member Countries.* World Bank. Washington, D.C.

Srinivasan, T.N. *The Costs and Benefits of Being a Small Remote, Island, Landlocked or Mini-state Economy.*

Van Wijnbergen, S. 1985. *Aid, Export Promotion and the Real Exchange Rate: An African Dilemma.* CPD Working Paper No. 1985-54, World Bank, Washington, D.C.

Wijeweera, Bernard S. 1992. *Public Administration in the Small Developing State: A Critique of the Theory,* International Review of Administrative Sciences, Vol. 58, London.

World Bank. 1991a. *World Development Report.* Washington, D.C.

_____. 1991b. *Pacific Island Economies: Towards Higher Growth in the 1990s. Washington, D.C.*

_____. 1992c. *Governance and Development.* Washington, D.C.

_____. 1993d. *Pacific Island Economies: Towards Efficient and Sustainable Growth* (in nine Volumes). Washington, D.C.

_____. 1994e. *Governance, The World Bank's Experience.* Washington, D.C.

_____. 1994f. *Health Priorities and Options in the World Bank's Pacific Island Member Countries.* Washington, D.C.

_____. 1995g. *Pacific Island Economies: Building a Resilient Economic Base for the Twenty-First Century.* Washington, D.C.

_____. 1996h. *From Plan to Market,* World Development Report, Washington, D.C.

_____. 1997i. *World Development Report*. Washington, D.C.

Role of Goverment

ADB. 1997. V*anuatu: The Comprehensive Reform Program* presented by the Republic of Vanuatu to the Consultative Group Meeting, Noumea, New Caledonia.

Barro, R. J. 1996. *Democracy and Economic Growth;* Journal of Economic Gowth, January.

Cooter, R. D. 1997. *The Rule of State Law Versus the Rule-of-Law State: Economic Analysis of the Legal Foundations of Development* in *Proceedings of the Annual World Bank Conference on Development Economics 1996,* Washington, D.C. World Bank.

Economic Insights Pty. Ltd. 1995. *The Economy of Fiji: Supporting Private Investment,* AusAID International Development Issues No. 40, Commonwealth of Australia, Canberra.

Fairbairn, T. I. J. and D. Worrell. 1996. *South Pacific and Caribbean Island Countries: A Comparative Study,* Foundation for Development Cooperation, Brisbane.

Government of the Republic of Fiji. 1993. *Opportunities for Growth: Policies and Strategies for Fiji in the Medium Term.*

Johnston, M. 1997. What Can Be Done About Entrenched State Corruption, in *Proceedings of the Annual World Bank Conference on Development Economics 1997,* Washington, D.C.: World Bank.

Kaku, M. (1997). *Visions: How Science will Revolutionize the 21st Century.*

Klitgaard, R. 1996. *Cleaning Up and Invigorating the Civil Service,* World Bank Operations Evaluation Department.

North, D. C. 1990. *Institutions, Institutional Change and Economic Performance,* Cambridge University Press.

Sachs, J. D. and A.M. Warner. 1995. *Economic Convergence and Economic Policies,* NBER Working Paper No. 5039, National Bureau of Economic Research, Cambridge, MA.

Siwatibau, S. 1997. *Strategic Planning and the Decision Making Machinery for National Development in Fiji,* mimeo.

Schoeffel, P. 1996. *Sociocultural Issues and Economic Development in the Pacific Islands,* Pacific Studies Series, Asian Development Bank, Manila, Philippines.

Solomon Islands Government. 1997. *Framework of Policy and Structural Reform Program,* Ministry of National Planning and Development and the Prime Minister's Office.

SPREP (South Pacific Regional Environment Programme). 1996. *State of the Environment Reporting for the Pacific.*

UNDP (United Nations Development Programme). 1997. *Review of Aid Coordination and Management in Fiji,* RAS/95/800 - Strengthening Aid Coordination and Management Capacity in Pacific Countries.

World Bank. 1995a. *Bureacrats in Business: The Economics and Politics of Government Ownership* Policy Research Report, Washington, D.C.

_____. 1996b. *Public Sector Modernization in the Caribbean,* Report No. 15185-CRG, Caribbean Division, Country Department III, Latin America and the Caribbean, Washington, D.C.

_____. 1997c. *The State in a Changing World,* World Development Report, Washington, D.C.

_____. 1997d. *Helping Countries Combat Corruption: The Role of the World Bank,* World Development Report, Washington, D.C.

Public Expenditure

AusAID. 1994. *Papua New Guinea, The Role of Government in Economic Development,* Report by Economic Insights Pty. Ltd.

Bierman, Hjordis,(Forthcoming) *Guidelines for Public Expenditure Review Missions to the Pacific Islands, FY1998,* July 1997.

Devarajan S., Swaroop V. and Zou H. *The Composition of Public Expenditure and Economic Growth,* Forthcoming in the Journal of Monetary Economics.

de Melo, Martha. 1988. *"Public Investment/Expenditure Reviews: The Bank's Experience."* World Bank, Public Economics Division, Country Economics Department, Washington, D.C.

International Monetary Fund. *Government Financial Statistics: Yearbook.* Washington, D.C.

Pradhan, Sanjay. 1996. *Evaluating Public Spending: A Framework for Public Expenditure Reviews.* World Bank Discussion Paper Series #323. Washington, D.C.: World Bank.

Pradhan, Sanjay. 1995. *Evaluating Broad Allocations of Public Spending: A Methodological and Data Framework for Public Expenditure Reviews.* World Bank, Public Economics Division, Policy Research Department, Washington, D.C.

World Bank. 1995. *"Review of Public Expenditure Work."* Office of the Vice President, Development Economics, Washington, D.C.

World Bank. 1996a. *Public Sector Modernization in the Caribbean,* Report No. 15185-CR4.

_____. 1997b. *The Public Expenditure Hand Book.*

Participation

Carvalho, S. and White, H. 1997. *Combining the Quantitative and Qualitative Approaches to Poverty Measurement and Analysis: the Practice and the Potential,* World Bank Technical Paper No. 366, Washington, D.C.

Holland J. and J. Blackburn, eds. 1997. *Whose Voice? Participatory Research and Policy Change,* Intermediate Technology Group, Rugby.

Rietbergen-McCracken, J. and Narayan D. 1997. *Participatory Tools and Techniques: A Resource Kit for Participation and Social Assessments.* Washington, D.C.: World Bank.

Robb, C. (forthcoming), *Is Local Knowledge Legitimate? Influencing Policy Through Participarory Poverty Assessment.* Washington, D.C.: World Bank.

Salem, C. and Robb, C. (forthcoming), *Participation for Portfolio Improvement: From Stakeholder Analysis to a Participation Plan.* Washington, D.C.: World Bank.

Salmen, Lawrence F. 1987. *Listen to the People,* A World Bank Publication.

_____. 1995. *Beneficiary Assessment: An Approach Described,* Environment Department Paper 023, Washington, D.C: World Bank.

_____. 1997. *Towards a Listening Bank, A Review of Best Practices and the Efficacy of Beneficiary Assessment.* Washington, D.C.: World Bank.

World Bank. 1994. *The World Bank and Participation,* Operations Policy Department, Washington, D.C.

World Bank. 1996 *Participation Source Book.*

Distributors of World Bank Publications

Prices and credit terms vary from country to country. Consult your local distributor before placing an order.

ARGENTINA
Oficina del Libro Internacional
Av. Córdoba 1877
1120 Buenos Aires
Tel: (54 1) 815-8354
Fax: (54 1) 815-8156
E-mail: olilibro@satlink.com

AUSTRALIA, FIJI, PAPUA NEW GUINEA, SOLOMON ISLANDS, VANUATU, AND SAMOA
D.A. Information Services
648 Whitehorse Road
Mitcham 3132
Victoria
Tel: (61) 3 9210 7777
Fax: (61) 3 9210 7788
E-mail: service@dadirect.com.au

AUSTRIA
Gerold and Co.
Weihburggasse 26
A-1011 Wien
Tel: (43 1) 512-47-31-0
Fax: (43 1) 512-47-31-29

BANGLADESH
Micro Industries Development
Assistance Society (MIDAS)
House 5, Road 16
Dhanmondi R/Area
Dhaka 1209
Tel: (880 2) 326427
Fax: (880 2) 811188

BELGIUM
Jean De Lannoy
Av. du Roi 202
1060 Brussels
Tel: (32 2) 538-5169
Fax: (32 2) 538-0841

BRAZIL
Publicações Tecnicas Internacionais Ltda.
Rua Peixoto Gomide, 209
01409 Sao Paulo, SP.
Tel: (55 11) 259-6644
Fax: (55 11) 258-6990
E-mail: postmaster@pti.uol.br

CANADA
Renouf Publishing Co. Ltd.
5369 Canotek Road
Ottawa, Ontario K1J 9J3
Tel: (613) 745-2665
Fax: (613) 745-7660
E-mail: order.dept@renoufbooks.com

CHINA
China Financial & Economic
Publishing House
8, Da Fo Si Dong Jie
Beijing
Tel: (86 10) 6333-8257
Fax: (86 10) 6401-7365

China Book Import Centre
P.O. Box 2825
Beijing

COLOMBIA
Infoenlace Ltda.
Carrera 6 No. 51-21
Apartado Aereo 34270
Santafé de Bogotá, D.C.
Tel: (57 1) 285-2798
Fax: (57 1) 285-2798

COTE D'IVOIRE
Center d'Edition et de Diffusion Africaines (CEDA)
04 B.P. 541
Abidjan 04
Tel: (225) 24 6510;24 6511
Fax: (225) 25 0567

CYPRUS
Center for Applied Research
Cyprus College
6, Diogenes Street, Engomi
P.O. Box 2006
Nicosia
Tel: (357 2) 44-1730
Fax: (357 2) 46-2051

CZECH REPUBLIC
USIS, NIS Prodejna
Havelkova 22
130 00 Prague 3
Tel: (420 2) 2423 1486
Fax: (420 2) 2423 1114

DENMARK
SamfundsLitteratur
Rosenoerns Allé 11
DK-1970 Frederiksberg C
Tel: (45 31) 351942
Fax: (45 31) 357822

ECUADOR
Libri Mundi
Libreria Internacional
P.O. Box 17-01-3029
Juan Leon Mera 851
Quito
Tel: (593 2) 521-606; (593 2) 544-185
Fax: (593 2) 504-209
E-mail: librimu1@librimundi.com.ec

CODEU
Ruiz de Castilla 763, Edif. Expocolor
Primer piso, Of. #2
Quito
Tel/Fax: (593 2) 507-383; 253-091
E-mail: codeu@impsat.net.ec

EGYPT, ARAB REPUBLIC OF
Al Ahram Distribution Agency
Al Galaa Street
Cairo
Tel: (20 2) 578-6083
Fax: (20 2) 578-6833

The Middle East Observer
41, Sherif Street
Cairo
Tel: (20 2) 393-9732
Fax: (20 2) 393-9732

FINLAND
Akateeminen Kirjakauppa
P.O. Box 128
FIN-00101 Helsinki
Tel: (358 0) 121 4418
Fax: (358 0) 121-4435
E-mail: akatilaus@stockmann.fi

FRANCE
World Bank Publications
66, avenue d'Iéna
75116 Paris
Tel: (33 1) 40-69-30-56/57
Fax: (33 1) 40-69-30-68

GERMANY
UNO-Verlag
Poppelsdorfer Allee 55
53115 Bonn
Tel: (49 228) 949020
Fax: (49 228) 217492
E-mail: unoverlag@aol.com

GHANA
Epp Books Services
P.O. Box 44
TUC
Accra

GREECE
Papasotiriou S.A.
35, Stournara Str.
106 82 Athens
Tel: (30 1) 364-1826
Fax: (30 1) 364-8254

HAITI
Culture Diffusion
5, Rue Capois
C.P. 257
Port-au-Prince
Tel: (509) 23 9260
Fax: (509) 23 4858

HONG KONG, CHINA; MACAO
Asia 2000 Ltd.
Sales & Circulation Department
Seabird House, unit 1101-02
22-28 Wyndham Street, Central
Hong Kong
Tel: (852) 2530-1409
Fax: (852) 2526-1107
E-mail: sales@asia2000.com.hk

HUNGARY
Euro Info Service
Margitszgeti Europa Haz
H-1138 Budapest
Tel: (36 1) 350 80 24, 350 80 25
Fax: (36 1) 350 90 32
E-mail: euroinfo@mail.matav.hu

INDIA
Allied Publishers Ltd.
751 Mount Road
Madras - 600 002
Tel: (91 44) 852-3938
Fax: (91 44) 852-0649

INDONESIA
Pt. Indira Limited
Jalan Borobudur 20
P.O. Box 181
Jakarta 10320
Tel: (62 21) 390-4290
Fax: (62 21) 390-4289

IRAN
Ketab Sara Co. Publishers
Khaled Eslamboli Ave., 6th Street
Delafrooz Alley No. 8
P.O. Box 15745-733
Tehran 15117
Tel: (98 21) 8717819; 8716104
Fax: (98 21) 8712479
E-mail: ketab-sara@neda.net.ir

Kowkab Publishers
P.O. Box 19575-511
Tehran
Tel: (98 21) 258-3723
Fax: (98 21) 258-3723

IRELAND
Government Supplies Agency
Oifig an tSoláthair
4-5 Harcourt Road
Dublin 2
Tel: (353 1) 661-3111
Fax: (353 1) 475-2670

ISRAEL
Yozmot Literature Ltd.
P.O. Box 56055
3 Yohanan Hasandlar Street
Tel Aviv 61560
Tel: (972 3) 5285-397
Fax: (972 3) 5285-397

R.O.Y. International
PO Box 13056
Tel Aviv 61130
Tel: (972 3) 5461423
Fax: (972 3) 5461442
E-mail: royil@netvision.net.il

Palestinian Authority/Middle East
Index Information Services
P.O.B. 19502 Jerusalem
Tel: (972 2) 6271219
Fax: (972 2) 6271634

ITALY
Licosa Commissionaria Sansoni SPA
Via Duca Di Calabria, 1/1
Casella Postale 552
50125 Firenze
Tel: (55) 645-415
Fax: (55) 641-257
E-mail: licosa@ftbcc.it

JAMAICA
Ian Randle Publishers Ltd.
206 Old Hope Road, Kingston 6
Tel: 876-927-2085
Fax: 876-977-0243
E-mail: irpl@colis.com

JAPAN
Eastern Book Service
3-13 Hongo 3-chome, Bunkyo-ku
Tokyo 113
Tel: (81 3) 3818-0861
Fax: (81 3) 3818-0864
E-mail: orders@svt-ebs.co.jp

KENYA
Africa Book Service (E.A.) Ltd.
Quaran House, Mfangano Street
P.O. Box 45245
Nairobi
Tel: (254 2) 223 641
Fax: (254 2) 330 272

KOREA, REPUBLIC OF
Daejon Trading Co. Ltd.
P.O. Box 34, Youida, 706 Seoun Bldg
44-6 Youido-Dong, Yeongchengpo-Ku
Seoul
Tel: (82 2) 785-1631/4
Fax: (82 2) 784-0315

LEBANON
Librairie du Liban
P.O. Box 11-9232
Beirut
Tel: (961 9) 217 944
Fax: (961 9) 217 434

MALAYSIA
University of Malaya Cooperative
Bookshop, Limited
P.O. Box 1127
Jalan Pantai Baru
59700 Kuala Lumpur
Tel: (60 3) 756-5000
Fax: (60 3) 755-4424
E-mail: umkoop@tm.net.my

MEXICO
INFOTEC
Av. San Fernando No. 37
Col. Toriello Guerra
14050 Mexico, D.F.
Tel: (52 5) 624-2800
Fax: (52 5) 624-2822
E-mail: infotec@rtn.net.mx

Mundi-Prensa Mexico S.A. de C.V.
c/Rio Panuco, 141-Colonia Cuauhtemoc
06500 Mexico, D.F.
Tel: (52 5) 533-5658
Fax: (52 5) 514-6799

NEPAL
Everest Media International Services (P) Ltd.
GPO Box 5443
Kathmandu
Tel: (977 1) 472 152
Fax: (977 1) 224 431

NETHERLANDS
De Lindeboom/InOr-Publicaties
P.O. Box 202, 7480 AE Haaksbergen
Tel: (31 53) 574-0004
Fax: (31 53) 572-9296
E-mail: lindeboo@worldonline.nl

NEW ZEALAND
EBSCO NZ Ltd.
Private Mail Bag 99914
New Market
Auckland
Tel: (64 9) 524-8119
Fax: (64 9) 524-8067

NIGERIA
University Press Limited
Three Crowns Building Jericho
Private Mail Bag 5095
Ibadan
Tel: (234 22) 41-1356
Fax: (234 22) 41-2056

NORWAY
NIC Info A/S
Book Department, Postboks 6512 Etterstad
N-0606 Oslo
Tel: (47 22) 97-4500
Fax: (47 22) 97-4545

PAKISTAN
Mirza Book Agency
65, Shahrah-e-Quaid-e-Azam
Lahore 54000
Tel: (92 42) 735 3601
Fax: (92 42) 576 3714

Oxford University Press
5 Bangalore Town
Sharae Faisal
PO Box 13033
Karachi-75350
Tel: (92 21) 446307
Fax: (92 21) 4547640
E-mail: ouppak@TheOffice.net

Pak Book Corporation
Aziz Chambers 21, Queen's Road
Lahore
Tel: (92 42) 636 3222; 636 0885
Fax: (92 42) 636 2328
E-mail: pbc@brain.net.pk

PERU
Editorial Desarrollo SA
Apartado 3824, Lima 1
Tel: (51 14) 285380
Fax: (51 14) 286628

PHILIPPINES
International Booksource Center Inc.
1127-A Antipolo St, Barangay, Venezuela
Makati City
Tel: (63 2) 896 6501; 6505; 6507
Fax: (63 2) 896 1741

POLAND
International Publishing Service
Ul. Piekna 31/37
00-677 Warzawa
Tel: (48 2) 628-6089
Fax: (48 2) 621-7255
E-mail: books%ips@ikp.atm.com.pl

PORTUGAL
Livraria Portugal
Apartado 2681, Rua Do Carmo 70-74
1200 Lisbon
Tel: (1) 347-4982
Fax: (1) 347-0264

ROMANIA
Compani De Librarii Bucuresti S.A.
Str. Lipscani no. 26, sector 3
Bucharest
Tel: (40 1) 613 9645
Fax: (40 1) 312 4000

RUSSIAN FEDERATION
Isdatelstvo <Ves Mir>
9a, Kolpachniy Pereulok
Moscow 101831
Tel: (7 095) 917 87 49
Fax: (7 095) 917 92 59

SINGAPORE; TAIWAN, CHINA; MYANMAR; BRUNEI
Ashgate Publishing Asia Pacific Pte. Ltd.
41 Kallang Pudding Road #04-03
Golden Wheel Building
Singapore 349316
Tel: (65) 741-5166
Fax: (65) 742-9356
E-mail: ashgate@asianconnect.com

SLOVENIA
Gospodarski Vestnik Publishing Group
Dunajska cesta 5
1000 Ljubljana
Tel: (386 61) 133 83 47; 132 12 30
Fax: (386 61) 133 80 30
E-mail: repansekj@gvestnik.si

SOUTH AFRICA, BOTSWANA
For single titles:
Oxford University Press Southern Africa
Vasco Boulevard, Goodwood
P.O. Box 12119, N1 City 7463
Cape Town
Tel: (27 21) 595 4400
Fax: (27 21) 595 4430
E-mail: oxford@oup.co.za

For subscription orders:
International Subscription Service
P.O. Box 41095
Craighall
Johannesburg 2024
Tel: (27 11) 880-1448
Fax: (27 11) 880-6248
E-mail: iss@is.co.za

SPAIN
Mundi-Prensa Libros, S.A.
Castello 37
28001 Madrid
Tel: (34 1) 431-3399
Fax: (34 1) 575-3998
E-mail: libreria@mundiprensa.es

Mundi-Prensa Barcelona
Consell de Cent, 391
08009 Barcelona
Tel: (34 3) 488-3492
Fax: (34 3) 487-7659
E-mail: barcelona@mundiprensa.es

SRI LANKA, THE MALDIVES
Lake House Bookshop
100, Sir Chittampalam Gardiner Mawatha
Colombo 2
Tel: (94 1) 32105

SWEDEN
Wennergren-Williams AB
P.O. Box 1305
S-171 25 Solna
Tel: (46 8) 705-97-50
Fax: (46 8) 27-00-71
E-mail: mail@wwi.se

SWITZERLAND
Librairie Payot Service Institutionnel
Côtes-de-Montbenon 30
1002 Lausanne
Tel: (41 21) 341-3229
Fax: (41 21) 341-3235

ADECO Van Diermen EditionsTechniques
Ch. de Lacuez 41
CH1807 Blonay
Tel: (41 21) 943 2673
Fax: (41 21) 943 3605

THAILAND
Central Books Distribution
306 Silom Road
Bangkok 10500
Tel: (66 2) 235-5400
Fax: (66 2) 237-8321

TRINIDAD & TOBAGO AND THE CARRIBBEAN
Systematics Studies Ltd.
St. Augustine Shopping Center
Eastern Main Road, St. Augustine
Trinidad & Tobago, West Indies
Tel: (868) 645-8466
Fax: (868) 645-8467
E-mail: tobe@trinidad.net

UGANDA
Gustro Ltd.
PO Box 9997, Madhvani Building
Plot 16/4 Jinja Rd.
Kampala
Tel: (256 41) 251 467
Fax: (256 41) 251 468
E-mail: gus@swiftuganda.com

UNITED KINGDOM
Microinfo Ltd.
P.O. Box 3, Alton, Hampshire GU34 2PG
England
Tel: (44 1420) 86848
Fax: (44 1420) 89889
E-mail: wbank@ukminfo.demon.co.uk

The Stationery Office
51 Nine Elms Lane
London SW8 5DR
Tel: (44 171) 873-8400
Fax: (44 171) 873-8242

VENEZUELA
Tecni-Ciencia Libros, S.A.
Centro Cuidad Comercial Tamanco
Nivel C2, Caracas
Tel: (58 2) 959 5547; 5035; 0016
Fax: (58 2) 959 5636

ZAMBIA
University Bookshop, University of Zambia
Great East Road Campus
P.O. Box 32379
Lusaka
Tel: (260 1) 252 576
Fax: (260 1) 253 952

ZIMBABWE
Academic and Baobab Books (Pvt.) Ltd.
4 Conald Road, Graniteside
P.O. Box 567
Harare
Tel: 263 4 755035
Fax: 263 4 781913

E-mail: LHL@sri.lanka.net